A Commentary on
DANIEL

A Commentary on
DANIEL

David Pawson

Anchor Recordings

First published in Great Britain in 2016 by
Anchor Recordings Ltd
DPTT, Synegis House, 21 Crockhamwell Road,
Woodley, Reading RG5 3LE

**For more of David Pawson's teaching,
including DVDs and CDs, go to
www.davidpawson.com**

**FOR FREE DOWNLOADS
www.davidpawson.org**

**For further information, email
info@davidpawsonministry.org**

ISBN 978-1-911173-06-9

Printed by Lightning Source

Contents

This book is based on a series of talks. Originating as it does from the spoken word, its style will be found by many readers to be somewhat different from my usual written style. It is hoped that this will not detract from the substance of the biblical teaching found here.

As always, I ask the reader to compare everything I say or write with what is written in the Bible and, if at any point a conflict is found, always to rely upon the clear teaching of scripture.

David Pawson

INTRODUCTION

The book of the prophet Daniel is one of the most interesting parts of the Bible. I daresay that if you went to Sunday school as a child you have certainly heard about the lions' den; you have probably heard about the fiery furnace; you may possibly have heard about Belshazzar's feast, and yet all the stories that you know from Sunday school days come from the first six chapters of this book. It is the second half that is relatively unknown unless you were brought up among the Brethren.

The book of Daniel divides into two neat halves: chapters 1–6 and chapters 7–end. Chapters 1–6 give us just a few glimpses into seventy-five years in a man's life, starting with his birth in a palace and finishing as a white-haired old man in his late eighties or early nineties, being thrown to the lions. Somehow it never dawned on me that Daniel was quite as old as that when he was thrown to those lions – all the more marvellous his courage when he faced them.

So we are going to study the life of this man. Yet these chapters, like one of Shakespeare's historical plays, constantly shift from the individual to the nation to the international scene. You are looking at a few individuals at one moment, and the next time, you are looking at history being made, and Daniel was a man who helped to make history. His influence on the affairs of mankind has been profound, and we are going to ask why. This young man, whom we first see in his teens, probably aged about sixteen

– how did he become the man who outlived four kings, two empires, and helped to change the history of those nations?

It is when we come to the second half, chapters 7–end, that we get a big surprise. There is a major change. In the first half, Daniel is referred to in the third person: "he". Somebody has written up these events after they happened and has recorded them for us. But when we turn to the second half, we find that "he" changes to "I"—"I, Daniel...." So there is a change from those who wrote *about* Daniel to Daniel, himself writing. But the biggest change is this: chapters 1–6 is history written *after* it happened, but when you get to chapter 7, Daniel writes history *before* it happened, and that involves a miracle. No man can do that. Only God can do that because only God knows what is going to happen. One of the exciting things in the book of Daniel is to change from studying history written after the events happened to studying history written before the events happened. This is such a miracle that people who do not believe in miracles can't believe that Daniel wrote it. Indeed, so accurate are the predictions that came true in absolute detail (not all of them yet; some of them are still to come true) that you are left with the choice of two opinions: either God told this to Daniel and gave him the miraculous power of prediction, or the book of Daniel is a forgery written centuries later, after the events it records.

Many modern scholars have taken that second view and treat this book as a forgery – somebody using the name of Daniel to try and kid us that it was prophecy. For me, the Lord Jesus Christ has settled the issue for he spoke of Daniel the prophet and quoted from that second half, and himself put his mark on Daniel's authorship of those words. Let every scholar be proved a liar and let Jesus be true. So I am going to treat it exactly as the Bible presents it to us: as half of the book written after the events occurred and half of the book written before they occurred. The message of the book comes through loud and clear in both halves: *God is in charge of history*. Whether you look back into the past or forward into the future, God is on the throne.

The key phrase of this book may be found in chapter four, occurring three times: "The Most High rules in the kingdom of men." This is a tremendous encouragement to us as we hear the news each day, as we see the nations apparently in chaos, and turmoil, as we read one bit of bad news after another. The text to say to yourself as you read your paper tomorrow is, "The Most High rules in the kingdom of men."

He knows what is happening. He is in charge; he is on the throne. We don't need to worry that affairs have got out of hand. They have got out of men's hands, but they haven't got out of God's hand, and that is the message of Daniel. We see that this gave him the courage to face anything – because God was in charge. We see three young men who say "let it be known we're going to serve God." It is this consciousness that God is in charge of history that gives us courage to face anything that can happen to us.

That is by way of introduction to the book itself. Read it right through. We are going to study it chapter by chapter. You get a far better understanding of the Bible if you read big chunks and then study the little parts rather than just nibbling at it mouthful by mouthful.

1

KIDNAPPED TEENAGERS
Read Daniel 1

A. STRANGE SURROUNDINGS (1–7)
    1. Transported to a heathen land – not embittered
    2. Trained in a heathen university – not affected
B. COURTEOUS COURAGE (8–16)
    1. Did the right thing
    2. In the right way
C. REMARKABLE RESULT (17–21)
    1. Academic studies
    2. Supernatural gifts

This chapter covers the years in Daniel's life from about sixteen to nineteen, the most critical years in many lives – in fact, in everybody's life. These are the years when we draw our own standards, the years when we leave home, when we know how we have been brought up and have to make the fateful decision as to whether our parents were right or wrong in giving us their guidelines. So in our adolescence, often thrown out into a strange world, away from the upbringing, away from the church in which we have been a child in Sunday school, we are alone and we decide during these years how we are going to live for the rest of our life. The decisions we make as teenagers are going to determine how we face any crisis in our nineties — that is the message of Daniel.

So we look at the background. I am dividing this chapter into three sections only. Verses 1–7, in which I want to say something about Daniel's strange surroundings, then verses 8–16, in which I want to think about Daniel's courteous courage (and I want you to notice both those words). Then finally, verses 17–21, Daniel's remarkable reward. These three things will sum up his teenage life.

First of all: Daniel's strange surroundings. Daniel had everything going for him. He was born with royal blood in his veins. He was as good-looking as you could hope to be. He was highly intelligent. He had a good education. He was all set to go to the top of the tree and would have been one of the aristocracy in his own land. One day, at the age of sixteen, he was taken off in chains to another land and he never came back. That is a pretty traumatic experience for a teenage lad.

The first verse of Daniel 1 states something that has

so frequented history and it can't get you excited: King Nebuchadnezzar invaded Israel and came and besieged Jerusalem. You could take any century in history and simply parallel that statement with the description of a large nation invading and swallowing up a small one. You could say, "In the second year of King George VI of England, Adolf Hitler invaded Czechoslovakia." That is just a statement of history. But when we look more closely into this first verse and the second verse, there are one or two unusual features that are rather different from other invasions.

The first is that Nebuchadnezzar came against *Jerusalem*. That is not the same thing as besieging London, New York, Tokyo or Moscow. He came against Jerusalem and that is God's place and it was God's people. What would God do? That is where the God who made the universe lived on earth. That is where his house was, and Nebuchadnezzar was attacking God's place. A man would need to be pretty bold to do that, but Nebuchadnezzar did it. Now here comes the most remarkable statement of all: *God gave him the victory* – no defence, no resistance, no protection. Nebuchadnezzar walked straight into Jerusalem and God let him. Oh God, what are you doing? I thought you were supposed to be a good God and these are your people; aren't you going to protect them, defend them? Why let this man come in? Why did God let Nebuchadnezzar in? Was it because Nebuchadnezzar was a good man? No, he was a tyrant. He loved to put people's eyes out; he loved to roast men alive. God gave victory to Nebuchadnezzar because Jehoiakim was a bad man, and Jehoiakim was the king of God's people.

Under the reign of Jehoiakim, which you can read about in the Bible, the permissive society came right into Jerusalem and the king did nothing about it. The result was that idolatry and immorality were staining God's people, and God warned them again and again. He was saying: If you go on like this, you'll have to leave this land. This is my land; this is the holy land. You can't live like this in this city. You go on like this and I'll take you to a land far away.

You know, they never took God seriously. They wouldn't listen to him, just as today people simply don't take the Word of God seriously. A man who walks through a crowd with a placard saying "Prepare to meet thy doom" will be laughed at, yet that is the Word of God and it needs to be listened to. The people of God didn't listen, and finally God's patience came to an end. The Lord gave victory to Nebuchadnezzar.

Winston Churchill, when he was called to the Admiralty at the beginning of the war, was invited to go and stay the night with the Prime Minister, who informed him of the appointment. When Churchill had been told, "You must take charge of the Admiralty," he went up to bed that night, and by the bedside the Prime Minister had put a Bible. Churchill opened that Bible and read just one verse from the Law of Moses before he went to bed. Paraphrasing, that verse referred to the time when God was telling Moses that when they got to Canaan they would drive out the people of Canaan before them. God said to Moses and the people of Israel through Moses: Don't you ever think that I am driving them out before you because you are better than them, I am driving them out because they are wicked. Churchill was told right there that night by God himself: Don't you think that if you win the war that is because you are better than they are; it is because I am dealing with their wickedness.

Did Nebuchadnezzar see that? Did Nebuchadnezzar say, "Thank you, Lord, for giving me the victory?" No fear! Nebuchadnezzar's attitude was: "Their God is nothing. My god is everything." He was still not at the stage of pride where he thought he was god. That comes a little later – in Daniel 4. He still worshipped a god himself. In fact, he worshipped many gods; he worshipped a god called Bel, another called Marduk and another called Aku, the moon god.

To teach the people a lesson and to tell the world that his god was the powerful one and had given them the victory, he went into the temple of God and took the sacred cups, the vessels that were used in the worship of God, and he packed them in his own luggage. He took them all the way back to Babylon and he set them up in the house of his god.

Archaeologists have unearthed a stone tablet on which were the words: "Nebuchadnezzar put the vessels of God in the house of his god." Archeology confirms the truth of even details in scripture, and that is what he did. Those vessels have a history. It is fascinating to follow them through. It is almost a sermon in itself. Years earlier, King Hezekiah of Judah had boastfully shown a previous king of Babylon those lovely gold vessels. I think he started something that day. I think word was passed down to subsequent kings that there were some lovely vessels over there in Jerusalem. Now Nebuchadnezzar took them. They are going to emerge again a few years later, when Belshazzar at his feast says, "Bring those vessels and we'll get drunk out of them." That was the last night he lived and reigned. Quite a story, those vessels, but it was a symbol of the fact that in Nebuchadnezzar's perverted mind, he thought that his god had given him the victory and that the God of Israel was nothing.

He never made a greater mistake in his life because, with the gold vessels, he took back to his own country some human vessels of God, men who were to announce his own downfall. He took with him some of the noble royal youths, to stop the royal line developing, to rob this nation of their leadership. He took back with him Daniel and three of Daniel's friends, and little dreamt that he was carrying the vessels of God right into his own territory.

Miles across the desert came this band of conquerors, with

the young men and the holy vessels, to the capital of Babylon, in which was one of the wonders of the world – the hanging gardens of Babylon. Its palace was a mighty place. When those young men came within sight of it, I guess their hearts might have sunk for a moment. They realised the power, the might and the glory of this conqueror. But in those four young men, God was coming to Babylon.

Centre of human pride, it had been built there by Nimrod. It had been built centuries earlier as a defiant act of rebellion against God. The tower of Babel (Babylon – same place). had been built up toward heaven to defy God and to worship the moon and the stars from its top. You can still see parts of that tower today. The remains show us that they worshipped the moon and the stars. They were astrologers trying to work out what the stars said.

Here is Daniel's teenage life. Nebuchadnezzar chose these four young men to be trained as his counsellors. It was a good move. He would be able to use them later to subdue their own nation. He would assimilate them into his royal court. He would bring fresh blood into his circle of counsellors. He liked the look of them. They were handsome; they were intelligent. He was always on the lookout for young men like that so he could surround himself with talent. Oh yes, it is all true to type and it is what many a ruler does. Of course, he could always use them as hostages. There are many reasons why he did it, but one thing he determined to do was so to brainwash them with the Babylonian culture that they would forget everything about their own land, their own people and their own God.

Nebuchadnezzar was an astute man, highly intelligent, and he realised their names would remind them of God. They must have had godly parents who loved God. There were two names for God in Israel: "El", and "I Am", or in Hebrew, "Yahweh" or "Yah" for short. Dani-*el*, Hanan-*yah*,

Misha-*el*, Azai-*yah*. Each of these boys had the name or title of God in his name.

So Nebuchadnezzar had to get rid of even that trace of their God. He changed their names, and into each of their new names he put one of their pagan gods from Babylon. There was the god Bel – Belteshazzar. "That's what you're called, Daniel." There was the god Aku, the moon god. "We will call you Shadraku. We will call you Mishahu." Then they had a god Nebo, or Nego, "We'll call you Abednego." Do you see how they changed the names? Let me give these names in English so you see the change. "Daniel" means, "God is Judge", and it was changed to "Bel" or "Baal, protect his life." "Hananiah" means "Yahweh is gracious", and it was changed to "Shadrach" – by command of Aku, the moon. "Mishael" means "Who is like God?" and they changed it to "Meshach", "Who is like Aku?" – the moon god. "Azariah" means "Yahweh is my helper" and they changed it to "Servant of Nego".

So they had obliterated every trace of these young men's upbringing and then sent them to university to learn cuneiform writing, to learn the Sumerian language, to be trained in science, mathematics, magic, astronomy and astrology – to go through the mill. They believed that when they came out at the other end they would be Babylonians.

There is something very relevant here. We think of the many young people who leave home (and maybe a church) and go to colleges and universities or to start a new job. This is a time when young people can go into an environment that is totally hostile to the Christian upbringing or church background they may have had. What is going to happen after three years? What is going to happen at the other end? How are they going to turn out? Does changing a name change someone's nature?

These are the strange surroundings in which Daniel and

these three other sixteen-year old lads found themselves. They had nothing but their memory to keep them straight. Would they survive? Many young people would not, under these pressures, but let us move on to the second thing: Daniel's courteous courage. I say to young Christians: There will come a point when you have left home, when you are away from your Christian environment. There will come one decision that is the key issue for you. There will come one matter in which you face a fork in the road, in which you can either do right or wrong, in which you can accept the way of God or the way of man. There will come some decision, maybe in your first few days away from home, but certainly in the first few months. Something will happen that faces you with this decision, and that key decision is going to affect you for the rest of your life. Make that one rightly and you will find the others are easier. Make a mistake at that point and you could be finished.

Now let us see what happened with Daniel and the three. Something came up for them in a surprising way: from the kitchen. Nebuchadnezzar wanted these young men fit, fat and well. He wanted them fed – as lambs to the slaughter almost – but he gave them the best of the food. He sent choice food down from his own table—"delicacies", we are told. He wanted to feed them up. That was how he lived and that was how he wanted them to live. For Daniel, this was the parting of the ways, the big issue.

Why should that be? He had accepted a university training that was far from godly; he had accepted a new name. Why was this the issue? Because this was the first thing that positively contradicted the commands of God. Why was the rich food wrong for Daniel? There are three possible reasons and let us look at them. One is the possibility that rich food is bad for a man of God anyway. I dare not say too much about this except to quote the great preacher Alexander

21

MacLaren, who once said, "Many dinner tables, over which God's blessing is formally asked, are spread in such a fashion as it is hard to suppose deserves his blessing." I leave that thought with you. Certainly, the Bible talks about gluttony as one form of self-indulgence, but I don't think that is the main reason here, though it could be a contributory factor. A second possibility is this: as a Jewish boy, Daniel was not allowed by God to touch meat with the blood in it or to eat flesh from unclean animals. But in a pagan court like Babylon, these unclean animals would certainly be eaten, and even clean animals would not be slaughtered in a kosher way.

A third possible reason comes out in the very interesting Persian word that is used for "food" here. It is a word that not only means "choice food", it also means "offering" or "tribute". In those days, before eating their food, people took the meat and offered it to their pagan gods, and so a meal became a sacrifice and the meat was offered to idols first. Daniel is not going to compromise here, and admit that these pagan gods are real.

Whatever the reason, the Bible doesn't say specifically, so you can take your choice between those three or accept all three of them; the point is this: Daniel knew in his conscience that if he took that meat he would be defiled. He would be dirty in God's sight, and therefore this was the decision. Praise God, Daniel, as a sixteen year old boy, made the right decision.

The second thing I want you to notice about this is not only his courage, but his *courtesy* in taking his stand. It is one thing to do the right thing, it is another thing to do it in the right way. It is one thing to have principles; it is another thing to be rude and aggressive about them. But Daniel not only made the right decision, he had the right attitude to other people. So while he was able to stand firm and be different from the others, he did not lose their respect – that is a very important point. He didn't say, "I'm not going to eat that meat and you can jolly well tell old Nebuchadnezzar I'm not." He didn't talk like that. So often, we Christians can take a stand at work, at the office party, or in something else in such a manner that we lose the respect, and therefore the relationship, that we have with people. We have done the right thing, but we have done it the wrong way.

Daniel was not rash, he was reasonable. He was not aggressive, he was approachable. So he went to Ashpenaz, the chief of Nebuchadnezzar's palace household. You can go to the British Museum today and there is a stone there and on it there is the inscription: "Ashpenaz, the chief of the eunuchs in the reign of King Nebuchadnezzar". There it is in the British Museum! People doubt whether Daniel is true – isn't it amazing?

Daniel went to Ashpenaz and to this man he said, "Look, I'm afraid I'm being asked to do something that is against my conscience. I am just putting in a formal request: could I please live on a vegetarian diet so I don't need to eat the meat?" He put it in as a request. He didn't say, "I'm jolly well not going to eat that meat." He said, "May I be excused from eating this meat?" – courteous, not rude, but poor Ashpenaz said, "It's as much as my life's worth. He will just have my head off if you fade away. You can't live on vegetables and water. No, I'm sorry. I can't give you your request."

Now what did Daniel do? Did he get all het up about it and did he start shouting at Ashpenaz? No, he quietly went to the waiter who served the meals and he said, "Do you mind coming to a little arrangement with me? Let's make a test. You just give me vegetables and water for ten days and let's see how we are at the end of that time." How reasonable, how courteous, and no wonder they had respect for Daniel. They saw that he was not only a man of God, but a gentleman. So the steward agreed to the test and you know what happened.

Ten days is rather short to test a diet. I think it showed that God was in it as well and doing something more than just the vegetables, but the fact is that at the end of it, those four young men stood out. They were fit and healthy. Now that is not saying that everyone has got to be vegetarian – don't let anybody run away with wrong ideas. The Bible allows you to eat meat as long as you don't offend the conscience of a weaker brother. There is nothing about vegetarianism being a Christian principle. But in this situation, it was right for Daniel not to eat meat, as Paul mentions other situations in which it is right not to. The result was that they were fit and well, they looked plumper, they had a better complexion, and so the test went on and they were allowed to continue. Now do you see an important lesson here? It is not just standing on your principles, it is doing it in the right way. It is not just being known to be different, it is being known to be different in such a way that you still keep in touch with people if you can. Let them cut themselves off from you, but don't you cut yourself off from them. Be courteous as well as courageous. Have your convictions, but live by them in a manner that is right and sensible. Daniel stands out as a man here who is not just right but wise, a man who knows how to do the right thing in the right way at the right time – that is wisdom.

Now look at the remarkable result. The time came for graduation, but before they could graduate they had to have their final exams, which in those days were always oral. In the case of these four young men, the king himself decided to conduct the examination for they were to become his advisers. He was grooming them for his council. So he interviewed these four men and he turned to his fellow examiners and said, "You know, they're ten times better than the others, aren't they?" Literally, he said, "They're ten hands higher." That was the way they expressed it in those days—ten times better. What a testimony that was!

I say to young people who are going away for training, if taking a course: part of your testimony for God could be those results in the exams – that is very practical. We can be so busy witnessing and doing other things that our studies are going down, but not Daniel. Daniel was at his best, and so he came out, having learned all the science, having learned all the knowledge that he could be given at that university, and he came out with flying colours in his exams.

But I will tell you something more: not only did he come out academically good, he came out with spiritual gifts as well as intellectual. God added to what he gained through the disciplined use of his own mind. God added other gifts, gifts of discernment and interpretation, so that he could do something that was very highly regarded in Babylon – he could interpret dreams and visions, for they believed a great deal in omens and messages through dreams and visions. This was going to be Daniel's main ministry through life. You can see he was such a good student that, in addition to his intellectual achievements, God gave him spiritual abilities. The two were to put Daniel right at the top.

What Britain desperately needs today is Christians right at the top, Christians in positions of responsibility. They will not get there by running straight off and witnessing but ignoring study and ignoring achievements that are possible within the human realm. They will get there by being the best at their job they can be. They will get there by going through the course, by coming out with flying colours, but not forgetting God – that God might add the spiritual qualities as well that will put them in those positions with a unique ministry. That is the message of Daniel.

Daniel wasn't thinking on a short term; he wasn't wanting to get the kingdom of God by next Thursday. He was going to be able to offer the Lord a lifetime. He would still be witnessing at ninety, so there were years of preparation, those three years of the Babylonian university, in a pagan environment, far away from the things of God, yet Daniel and his three friends stuck it out. They stayed with God and they came out of those exams fit to be appointed to positions of responsibility.

What a remarkable reward that this captive foreigner should become part of a king's council in a mighty empire. Like Benjamin Disraeli in a much later era, this Jew was to become a prime minister in a Gentile country. He was to be turned to by kings for advice. God knows what he is doing. God put this young man in the middle of a pagan empire because God is in control and God rules in the kingdoms of men.

In closing, I want to highlight how vital two stages in life are: childhood and adolescence. Childhood is the period when decisions are made for us, when parents tell us what is right and wrong, and when standards are set and the memory is filled with those standards. Daniel's very name, and the other three names, tell us that they had parents who knew God and who set the standards right. How vital that is. Thank God if you had a childhood like that, when you were given guidelines in your earliest years.

But the second key period is adolescence, when we decide for ourselves. It is a tragedy when young people simply decide not to go their parents' way for no better reason than that it is their parents' way. That is not a good enough reason. But how happy it is, what a wonderful thing it is, when a child who has been given the right standards as a child but is now on their own, away from home, in a hostile environment, says, "I'm still going to live like this because I believe it to be right. I believe it to be God's way for me."

So Daniel came through childhood and was then forcibly cut off from his background. No longer could it support him. Now he was on his own, which way would he turn? He resolved in his heart that he would not be defiled. Because he would not eat the king's meat when he was sixteen, the lions wouldn't eat him when he was ninety.

2

NEBUCHADNEZZAR'S NIGHTMARE
Read Daniel 2

A. IMPOTENCE OF MAN (1–24)
    1. Protest (1–12)
        a. Impossible demand
        b. Impending death
    2. Prayer (13–24)
        a. Beseeching grace
        b. Blessing God
B. OMNIPOTENCE OF GOD (25–49)
    1. Recollection (25–35)
        a. Deteriorating statue
        b. Destroying stone
    2. Revelation (36–49)
        a. Passing kingdoms
        b. Permanent king

DANIEL 2 : "NEBUCHADNEZZAR'S NIGHTMARE"

RULE

KINGDOM

① GOLD
Autocracy

BABYLONIAN
Nebuchadnezzar

② SILVER
Oligarchy

MEDO - PERSIAN
Cyrus, Darius, etc.

③ COPPER
Aristocracy

GRECIAN
Alexander, etc.

④ IRON
Republic

ROMAN
Julius Caesar, etc.

B.C
A.D

⑤ IRON + CLAY
Democracy
Dictatorship } Federacy (10)

EUROPEAN?
ARABIAN?
Antichrist?

v.

⑥ STONE

FIRST ADVENT?
SECOND ADVENT?
Christ

⑦ MOUNTAIN
Theocracy

CHURCH?
MILLENNIUM?
KINGDOM OF HEAVEN
God.

It is a comparatively recent discovery that most of us dream many times every night. Fortunately, we forget most of those dreams, and the ones we remember are most likely to be the ones we dreamt just before waking up, when we were semiconscious. Those dreams have an obvious and natural cause which we are now understanding. For example, some of your dreams are related to things that have happened to you during the day, and though the details get a bit muddled you can understand how you came to dream like that. Psychologists have suggested various theories and have tried to explore the meaning of dreams as a clue to our mental health and some of the problems that we are not willing to face.

But sometimes a dream does not have a natural cause. Occasionally, a dream is a supernatural thing and a way of God speaking to someone, for the simple reason that in their waking conscious life their mind would refuse such extraordinary truth. So when we are relaxed in bed, when we are not in conscious control of our thoughts, sometimes God is able to speak very clearly indeed about himself, about ourselves, and sometimes even about the future. That is why the Bible contains a number of dreams. Jacob's ladder is perhaps the best known, but there are many others. What about the two Josephs? Joseph in the Old Testament, a man of dreams about things that would come true; Joseph in the New Testament, the foster parent of Jesus. But for the dreams that Joseph had, Jesus would have been killed in the first few months of his life. So God can use dreams to speak and to reveal things yet to be.

This chapter two of Daniel, which is one of the longest chapters in the Bible, is entirely built around a nightmare, a terrifying dream that had a king trembling though he was the greatest world power that had ever yet been seen. He was trembling in his bed and he could not get to sleep again. He woke up in a cold sweat. Somehow he knew that it was a dream from beyond, a dream that had great significance for his future, containing within it tragedy and horror, a dream that he couldn't understand because, alas, it is probable that he couldn't remember it.

Have you ever woken up like that and thought, "That was a horrible dream and I can't for the life of me remember what it was about. I just have a vague feeling of dread and fear – there was something awful in that dream"? It is hard to get back to sleep because your mind teases over it. You may remember a detail here and a detail there, but somehow the whole thing has got lost. Nebuchadnezzar, at the peak of his career, lies sleepless on his bed until the morning—that is the background of this story. Within that dream, God was going to reveal the future to a pagan emperor as he had, for example, to Pharaoh centuries earlier.

This chapter presents us with the pattern of world history. Somebody has called it the "A, B, C of biblical prophecy". If you grasp this dream and its meaning you have a key to unlock the whole course of world history. It is perhaps the most important dream that anybody dreamed in the scripture from that point of view. We are going to explore it now, and we start at the beginning.

There are two lessons to be learned from this chapter. I divide it right down the middle, and in the first part of the chapter it seems that the great lesson is the impotence of man. With all our science, all our knowledge, all our education, all our understanding, there are certain questions we cannot answer. One of them is about the future. How is it all going to end? "What is the world coming to," we say to each other on the bus and in the office. Nobody knows except God, and he has revealed it in a dream, a nightmare, to Nebuchadnezzar.

So the impotence of men comes out in the first part, and yet, when you realise the limitations of your knowledge, when you realise that you don't know the answers, what do you do? There are two possibilities. One is to protest that these things are beyond the reach of the human brain, the other is to pray to God who knows everything, and seek wisdom from him. There are two things you can do when you are helpless, when you have come to the limit of your resources. One is to protest and give up and say, "I can go no further, this is an impossible situation, and I can do nothing in it," the other is to hold a prayer meeting. Four young men got down on their knees and prayed to the God of heaven.

They were acknowledging the impotence of men, but one group was acknowledging the omnipotence of God. That is what comes out in the second half of the chapter. The power, the sovereignty, the knowledge, the wisdom, the might – everything that God has, came through very clearly, both in recalling the past and in revealing the future. For only God knows what is unknown to man.

So let us look at the first part of the chapter, the first twenty-four verses. Nebuchadnezzar's dream, I have pointed out, had a supernatural origin but it also had a natural origin. It was related to the things he was thinking about when he went to bed. If you go to bed with things on your mind, they are things you are likely to dream about. When Nebuchadnezzar lay down that night he found himself reviewing his meteoric rise to the peak of his career – the most powerful world ruler, now he had no rival, no worlds left to conquer.

He lay on his bed that night before he went to sleep, well satisfied with the past but very much afraid of the future. It is the mark of a man who has arrived that he begins to get anxious about what is going to happen. Having come to the top of his career, now Nebuchadnezzar began to wonder how long he could hold that position, how long he could stay at the top. He knew that he was not there forever and that he must go down some day, and he began to wonder who would take over, and what would happen, and who would carry things on. So he went to bed wondering about the future, asking questions. This great Babylonian empire, the like of which had never been seen before – what would happen to it? So his dream did grow out of natural things, but naturally his dream could only have posed the questions. Supernaturally, his dream gave the answers.

Then he woke up in the early hours of the morning with a start. No doubt he got the wise men out of bed too, and the astrologers. You can hear them grumbling to their wives: "There's the old emperor. What's he want at this time of the morning?"

Up they get, and into his presence. "I've had a nightmare, a terrible dream. There's tragedy in it and I must know. Now come on, you're wise, I've trained you. I've given you the best of my food. I've spent my money on you. Tell me what the dream meant."

"Well, all right. You tell us what the dream was and we'll find an explanation for it." They didn't quite put it that way but that is what they meant.

Nebuchadnezzar said, "No, I'm not going to tell you."

Now the obvious reason why he didn't tell them could be that he had forgotten the dream. That is one interpretation I read, and it is a probable one. But I want to mention the other possible reason why he didn't give them the dream. The literal meaning is, "The word has gone from me," which normally is a phrase used by a king to denote a decision reached that can't be undone, something he has said he is going to stand by, rather than something that has gone from his memory.

So the possibility is that Nebuchadnezzar did remember that dream, at any rate in outline if not in detail. The basic reason why he is refusing to tell them the dream is this: he is testing their ability. If they have the ability to know the unknown future then they should also have the ability to know the unknown past. That is a very good test of someone who is going to tell you what is going to happen in the future: "Alright, if you know such things then you should know exactly what has happened to me in the past. Go right ahead, I'm listening."

So important was this dream to Nebuchadnezzar that he was going to be absolutely sure that they knew what they were talking about. So he puts them on the spot and says, "If you're so clever you ought to be able to tell me both the past and the future. Come on, you tell me the dream and its meaning, and then I'll know that you've got the ability to do such things." A very clever way to put them on the spot, if that is the meaning of the phrase. Either way, it was the test of whether they really could do what they had been paid to do.

The simple answer is that they couldn't. They pleaded for a bit more time and Nebuchadnezzar said, "I can see you are frauds; I can see what you are trying to do. You are trying to gain time so that something will happen and then I'll be out of the way and you won't need to tell me the dream. I can see through you." He was furious, frustrated and angry. So he ordered them all to be put to death, a very common occurrence in royal courts in those days.

But at least they were honest enough to say three things. First they said, "This is beyond our human intellect." True. Then they said, "You'll need gods to tell you this." Third, they said, "We're not in touch with the gods." In other words, they presented the king with a simple statement of fact, and they must have been pretty bold to do so. "We don't know; gods know; we're not in touch" – a very plain confession of their inability. No wonder Nebuchadnezzar was furious. They had lived from his pocket all their lives. They had had the best of everything in his court simply because they claimed to be able to give him advice when he needed it. Now, when the crunch came, they couldn't do a thing.

So they were sentenced to death and Arioch whose job it was to be the chief of the executioners (and what a comment on that empire that they had a chief of executioners – full time job) was told to go and round them up, not only to round up the wise men but round up their students also, because if the wise men couldn't speak in this situation then what was the point of keeping the students they were training? Among those students were four young men who had not been at the audience but now found themselves chained and led to the condemned cell.

Daniel said to Arioch very calmly, "What's up? Why has the king suddenly decided to do this? Why is he so angry?" You know, the calm of Daniel hits you square between the eyes. A man who is in the condemned cell who can say, "Tell us what it's all about; what's the matter?" is a man who has got control of himself, a man who is calm and has the poise of a man of God. He has courage too, to want to be involved with a king in a temper. So he is told by Arioch what the trouble is. Here is Daniel facing death at the age of nineteen and yet he is not panicking, he is not getting all worried about it. He simply says, "What's up? What's the matter? Why are we being condemned to death?"

When he is told, Daniel goes straight into the king and says, "Just give me a little time and I will tell you the dream." The confidence of this teenage boy – "I will tell you"! – knowing that if he failed, his death was not only certain but he would probably be tortured as well. Why did he ask for time? Because he had to go and consult someone. Some people just protest when they get to the end of human resources, some just sit down and resign themselves to their fate and say, "Well, we can't help it. We can't go any further." But some say, "There is a God in heaven, and man's extremity is God's opportunity. When we get to the end of what we can do, we're at the beginning of what he can do," and Daniel went to prayer.

They were honest in their motives for prayer. They prayed that God would save their lives. I want you to know two things about prayer now, and Daniel is a book of tremendous lessons in prayer. Study the prayers of Daniel. First, their prayer besought the grace of God. They asked God if, of his mercy, he would give them the dream. They did not say, "Lord, we have a right to have this." They did not say, "Lord, our lives depend on it." They said, "Lord, in your mercy, as an undeserved favour, would you give us this dream?" Every petition we bring to the Lord must be a petition for his mercy, an undeserved blessing.

I want you to notice that Daniel got three others to pray with him and the four prayed together. The power of united prayer! "If two or three are agreed on earth as touching anything," said Jesus, "your Father will do it." Just two or three – the power of two or three asking together. Not just getting together, he didn't ask three to come and listen to him praying. That is some people's idea of a prayer meeting but it wouldn't be Daniel's. If you go to a prayer meeting it should be to pray not to listen to others. He asked those three others to come and join him to pray, and they asked God. Each of those four, in the presence of the other three, asked God for this thing. God loves people to ask for things together in each other's presence, and he loves them all to pray together. Believe me, churches are strong not just when individuals within them pray but when they get together to pray – that is when God moves.

So they had a prayer meeting and they prayed together. But only one of the four received what they prayed for—and that is enough. When we gather together in a church to pray, we should be quite happy if the answer to that prayer comes to just one person in the fellowship. God has answered and has given what was needed to help all who had prayed. That is so often the way that he works. When a fellowship asks for something, God anoints one person within that fellowship with the answer, to save and help the whole fellowship, and that is one of his patterns.

After they had besought the mercy of God in the prayer meeting, Daniel lay awake that night. It could have been his last night on earth but he lay awake. He didn't dream, he had a vision, which means he saw a picture while he was awake. A dream is a picture you see while you are asleep, and a vision is a picture you see while you are awake. He saw a vision and he knew the dream, and he understood.

Now I want you to notice that instead of rushing to the king with the answer, he went back on his knees to pray. Do you see that? Before ever he enjoyed the blessing of sharing the answered prayer he went back to say thank you. Here are two prayers, not one: the prayer of "please" and the prayer of "thank you" – the prayer of beseeching and the prayer of blessing; the prayer for grace and the prayer to God. In the second prayer, Daniel pours out his soul and he praises God that the answers come, and he has remembered to say thank you.

I remember a dear little old lady in Nottinghamshire. I was with the church of which she was a member for one month, taking various meetings. When we began that month, when we announced a prayer meeting, I and my colleague were joint evangelists in a caravan, and when we began that series of meetings we invited people to come and pray. This dear little old lady was the only one who came for quite some time at the beginning. Every morning at ten o'clock she was there.

The thing that she taught us in prayer was this: she was a little soul but she had big faith and she would pray for things and she would never finish the prayer without saying "Thank you" for them. I never quite heard that again since, but this little lady said, "Lord, we ask for this and thank you so much for it." Her faith always said "thank you" before the blessing came. She didn't wait for it, she just said thank you. You can guess what that woman's prayers did for those meetings.

Daniel went back on his knees straightaway. "Oh God of my fathers, thank you." His prayer was first of all a prayer *about* God and then a prayer *to* God. About God as he is: God who has all wisdom and all power and sovereignty and might; and then God as he shares things with us. Thank you for giving me your wisdom and your knowledge – a prayer that had no please in it at all, just thank you, thank you, thank you. God loves praise. He wants us to pray together first and then he wants us to praise him together for what he has done.

If you are like that, you will be able to go to any king with an answer – or anyone at all. You are able to go to any situation with something from God for that situation.

We now turn to the second half of the chapter. Something now comes out which may not strike you as funny but I find it hilarious. Arioch, the chief executioner, says, "I have found a man" – a typical little bureaucrat! "I have found someone" – he wants to get all the credit for himself. It wasn't he who found someone. Daniel had spoken to Arioch. But Arioch came strutting into the king's presence. Was he hoping for a little promotion? What a funny little man.

In contrast to Arioch who was trying to get the credit, we see Daniel refusing to take the credit. It is a little point but it is there. Arioch says, "I've found a man who has the answer."

The king says to Daniel, "Can you tell me?"

Daniel says, "No man can tell you." I would have thought he might have said, "Yes," he had got the answer, but he didn't say, "Yes, I can," he said, "No man can tell you but there is a God in heaven who tells secrets."

You find that Daniel goes out of his way to see that God gets the glory for this. Even if God has given us the answer, even if God has given us a gift for someone else to pass on, even if he has given us the solution to the problem, we should never say, "I've got the solution." We should say, "There's a God in heaven who tells secrets."

So Daniel is first of all able to recollect the entire dream, and able to tell Nebuchadnezzar everything about it. Let us run quickly through it. The dream is made up of two parts, a statue and a stone, and the stone destroys the statue. That is the simplest outline of the dream. The statue is a huge, towering, terrifying figure. I think this statue appeared to the king to be about ninety feet high. He lay in bed and he saw this huge giant towering above him. It was shining and it was close to him, and he could just see the face looking right up. The head was gold, the chest and arms were silver, and the belly and the thighs were brass. Incidentally, that would have been copper; they didn't have brass alloy in those days. It is a mistranslation. It would be polished copper. Then iron legs and then feet, and the most surprising feature: feet of clay and iron mixed together. Now that would not mean wet clay that would mean tile or pottery, baked clay. Yet baked clay and iron wouldn't just hold together very well; they are a funny mixture. As you go down from the head to the feet, one thing increases, namely hardness – from gold through silver to copper and iron, and iron and clay. I want you to notice three things however that go down. *Value* goes down. These metals are increasingly less precious. *Weight* goes down (gold is heaviest), and *brilliance* goes down. The shining goes down as you go down the whole statue.

I want you to notice that the feet are the weakest part, the most brittle, the most easily smashed.

Then in the dream there is a stone that has not been cut by man but that clearly is a natural stone, a rock that has been cut by some supernatural agency, that comes bursting out of nowhere and strikes the weakest part of the image. The whole thing collapses into tiny pieces and vanishes. The stone is left standing there and then the stone gets bigger and bigger until it covers the whole earth and is a mighty mountain—that is the dream. Nebuchadnezzar, as he listened to this, must have been absolutely astonished. Daniel went straight on and said, "That's the dream, now I'll tell you what it means." From recollection we have the miracle of revelation.

It was the answer to Nebuchadnezzar's thoughts about the future. The statue represented the passing kingdoms and empires of men, four of them in particular.

"Nebuchadnezzar, you are the head." I have examined various photographs in the British Museum and elsewhere and I have an illustration of the head of Nebuchadnezzar, showing his crown; and an off the shoulder robe – in fact a copy of the robe of Darius, king of the Medo-Persian Empire; a tunic I copied from a picture of Alexander the Great, the Grecian emperor; then we come down to the Roman legs and sandals.

Those illustrations must have been very like the image that he saw, though the latter would have been much more frightening. "Nebuchadnezzar you are the head. You are the most brilliant of these empires. You are the gold. God has given you this kingdom." Notice: "God has given it to you" – even though Nebuchadnezzar was a despot. "And after you there is going to be another empire," and the two arms folded would represent two parts united. In fact, the next empire was the empire of the Medes and the Persians making laws together. After that came Alexander the Great, who in eleven short years conquered every known part of his world and sat down weeping because there were no more worlds to conquer, and he died at thirty-three of debauchery – the empire of Greece. After that came the empire of Rome, and how symbolic it was: legs marching, trampling, crushing, and Rome marched through the world and extended the empire greater than ever before—such is the meaning.

Now what do the feet mean? I'm going to leave that for the time being because I want to come back to it. I just want you to notice that none of these other empires was in existence at the time that Nebuchadnezzar dreamed. The Medes and the Persians were just little areas within his empire. In Greece there were only wandering tribes. In Rome there was only a little village on the Tiber. Yet God, who knows the future, knew that these unknowns would arise as mighty empires, world kingdoms.

Now in what way did these later kingdoms deteriorate? In what way are they inferior to Nebuchadnezzar? The only answer I can come to, though I am not going to be too dogmatic on this, I will leave you to judge for yourself, is this: that in sovereignty, in rule, in government, they decline. Nebuchadnezzar had real rule; he was a king. What he said went and that is kingship – that is a kingdom. When it was the Medes and the Persians, the king had 120 governors to help him, and even the king was subject to the laws of the Medes and the Persians and could not change them. That is an oligarchy, whereas Nebuchadnezzar had an autocracy. In the Greek empire we had rule by the nobility, the aristocracy, and many people were raised from the ranks of the ordinary to the noble and began to share in government, moving towards democracy. Then in the Roman empire the emperor was chosen by popular vote and could be thrown out by popular vote.

In spite of those who think that democracy is the highest

NEBUCHADNEZZAR'S NIGHTMARE *Daniel 2*

form of government, in God's sight it is one of the lowest. When God made man he meant us to be subject to a king who actually ruled. Our own constitutional monarchy and what we dare to call a "United Kingdom" is an absolute travesty of kingship. Our royal family has little or no power, and it really is a dreadful decline from what God intended. So Nebuchadnezzar's government was the best in God's sight as a form of government. You see the deterioration until, finally, the toes, when we reach them, are an attempt to mix power and popularity. Iron and clay – the clay being the seed of men, we are told. So you get this strange mixture that we are living in today of democracy and dictatorship, overthrows, and constant instability of government. That is my interpretation – I will leave it with you for what it is worth.

History, like water, is running downhill. We are not rising, we are not progressing, we are not evolving, we are going downhill rapidly. Governments are going downhill. But praise God.

We will leave the feet for the moment. Let us go to something we do know – the stone, what is that? That will smash all human kingdoms to pieces and replace them. The stone is one of the titles of Jesus. You will find it again and again. There it is in Psalm 118, in Isaiah 8, in Matthew, and in Acts 4 and 1 Peter 2. All the way through, you find Jesus, the stone which the builders rejected, has been made the head of the corner: the chief cornerstone, the rock, our rock of ages. There is no doubt whatever as to what this stone represents: it is Christ, and our Christ will one day smash human civilisations and build in their place a kingdom that is the kingdom of God. That is my hope for the future and it is as certain as Nebuchadnezzar's nightmare and Daniel's interpretation of it.

So we look forward to the day when the kingdom of God

comes, and it is Christ who will bring it. It is Christ who smashes the kingdoms. But now we come to the closing difficulty of our study. When will this happen? When does Christ smash the kingdoms of the world? When is our prayer answered: "Thy kingdom come ... on earth as it is in heaven"? Here Christians have been divided between two answers. I give them both, and we must respect each other if we differ on them.

Some say it is when Jesus came to earth the first time. The kingdom of God broke through in him. That is true. He came to establish the kingdom of God and people could enter the kingdom – that is true. Those who enter the kingdom are growing in number and spreading throughout the world – that is true. But somehow it doesn't quite fit because the other empires are still there. There has been no confrontation between the church and the empire. There is no catastrophic collision in which human civilisation has disappeared and blown like chaff in the wind.

I don't think that is the full answer. So I turn to the other possible answer: when Jesus comes a second time. I believe this is the full answer. I find a remarkable truth in, for example, Daniel 7, and in Revelation 19 – that when our Lord returns to earth he will find in the centre of world affairs a federation of ten kingdoms and ten rulers. I don't think it is a coincidence that what the Lord smashes here are ten toes of man's world empires. If you read through Revelation 19, it is Christ as King of kings and Lord of lords who will smash that final form of human imperialism and replace the mess with the kingdom of heaven breaking in on earth.

I believe that once you take that interpretation it all fits, the whole thing makes sense. Which leaves just one more question to answer: if, then, the feet, the mixture of iron and clay – that part of human ambition and pride – is to be revealed in the last days, and indeed Daniel said to

Nebuchadnezzar, "God has told you what will come to pass in the latter days" – if this is right, then is there any sign in our day of these things happening?

Again Christians are saying two things at the moment and I pass them on to you for what they are worth. On the one hand are those who believe that the iron in those feet indicates a revived Roman Empire in Western Europe, and who see in the European Union an ominous portent of our days. There are those who believe that Europe is heading towards being these feet that Christ will smash. I think we must say that is human opinion and we must leave it there until the Lord makes things known more clearly.

But there is another possibility. When Rome fell, it fell first in the West, but not in the East until a thousand years after Christ. Who took over from Rome? In the area of the world in which God's purposes are worked out, the area that covers Babylon and Jerusalem, who took over? The answer is the Muslims took over; the Arab world took over. When you think in that direction, a new thought occurs: could it be that the Arabs descended from Abraham could be those who present the final challenge to the God of Israel? And could it be that we should look for ten nations of Arabs uniting together against God's people and therefore against God, and presenting the final challenge to the world? An uneasy federation of countries, some of which would be the iron of dictatorship and some the clay of democracy, but joined together in a federation to establish world power – could that be also? That again is human opinion.

Frankly, I can't make up my mind between these two or whether to look for a third possibility. I think what is clear is that we are not yet at the feet of this statue, and that when we are we shall be in no doubt whatever. It will fit in perfect detail every prediction that the Word of God makes. I do not yet see all these predictions coming true but I believe it is happening and that before our very eyes we shall see unfolding the purposes of God and the pride of human empire.

While prediction of events is fascinating and encourages our faith, chapter two takes us back to Daniel and Nebuchadnezzar. Was Nebuchadnezzar converted through this vision? No. He worshipped Daniel and he said "your God". It was not until he went mad (as we shall read in chapter four) that ultimately he realised sanity in God. So Nebuchadnezzar was not converted. God can speak to an unconverted person, and it doesn't convert that person.

Daniel was rewarded and lifted to a position of supreme authority in a pagan empire. But what magnanimity there was in his character. He said, "Nebuchadnezzar, I wouldn't have been able to tell you about this dream unless my three friends had prayed with me," and so his three friends shared the reward. That tells you something about Daniel. What about God who is the real hero of this story? He is the God who answers prayer, the God who reveals secrets, the God who knows the future, the God who saves lives, the God who controls history.

History is not chaos, not chance, it is going somewhere, and it is going where God wants it to go. The statue means one thing: that one day all human constructions will be destroyed, all human civilisations will vanish, all human kingdoms will go; and the stone means that one day the kingdom of God will come to stay.

3

THREE PLUS ONE IN THE FIRE
Read Daniel 3

A. TOTALITARIAN DOMINANCE (1–7)
    1. Symbolisation
    2. Unification
B. CONSCIENTIOUS DISOBEDIENCE (8–23)
    1. Accusation
    2. Condemnation
C. MIRACULOUS DELIVERANCE (24–30)
    1. Vindication
    2. Protection

This chapter, Daniel 3, has been a favourite with children in Sunday school and at many a bedtime, and I can remember in my childhood asking for the story of Shadrach, Meshach, and "Into-bed-you-go"! Yet this story, like most of the Bible, was not written for children but for adults. It is about a very adult situation, for these three were not young, they were now in their forties. They belonged to that age group that is one of the most godless of the male sex, when we are proud, when we are at the peak of our own powers, and before we have begun to realise that we are sliding down the wrong side of the hill.

So these men were mature, but they were not self-dependent. They trusted God and did what was right. This passage is concerned with the situation when obedience to God and obedience to men are in conflict, a situation that arises in many places in the world today where if men and women are going to obey God they must disobey people. It is in this kind of conflict under social pressure that these three men stood firm for God.

One of the puzzles of Daniel 3 is: where was Daniel? He was the leader of this bunch of four; Daniel had been at the Babylonian university with the three others. It was he who had led them and made decisions for them. It was he who had taken the stand and encouraged them to stand also. Now Daniel is not there. I presume that he was away on business for the king or just not around. These three are on their own now, without their leader. The glory of it is that Daniel had so led them that when he was gone they stood firm.

Let us begin by looking at the first seven verses. We could call the theme "Totalitarian Dominance". That is a big expression. Lord Acton's famous dictum "Power tends to corrupt and absolute power tends to corrupt absolutely" will always be true as long as there is human history. Power tends to go to a man's head. When he becomes boss, when he becomes an emperor, when he is top dog, the tragedy is that from top dog he turns that last word wrong way around and begins to think he is "top god". It is one of the things that happens to human nature. Most of us find power very difficult to control, and sooner or later it controls us.

Nebuchadnezzar was such a man, he had become top dog and so he thought he was top god. He began to do things that showed that he had stepped over the line of a human ruler to seeking to be a divine ruler. It began with a gigantic image or statue – we don't know what it looked like. Mind you, archaeologists believe they have found the remains of it. About six miles southeast of the site of ancient Babylon in the plain of Dura, which is just a vast flat clay basin with the hills in the distance, they found in the middle of that plain a brick base about forty-five feet square and some twenty feet high, solid brick, and clearly there has been something huge standing on it in the days of the Babylonian Empire, but there are no remains of that now. Was this the pedestal? If so, then it could be seen for twelve to fifteen miles. Covered with gold leaf, it would glint in the sun, the rising sun would catch the head of it even before the sunshine was seen down on the ground. You can get the picture of this gigantic thing, ninety feet high and nine feet wide, very tall and very slim – not human proportions so it may be doubted whether it was strictly a human figure. It might just have been an obelisk. We just don't know. So this gigantic statue, put up in the plain – what was its meaning? I mentioned its dimensions in feet, but in fact they didn't measure it by feet, it was sixty cubits by six. I want you to note that figure very carefully. Throughout the Bible, seven is the number of perfection, the number of God, and it means that which is complete and perfect. The number throughout the Bible for man is always six. All his efforts always fall short of perfection and therefore man's number is six. That is why one day there will come a world ruler to our world whose number will be "666". It signifies the glory and the power of man. Undoubtedly, this is what this obelisk was for. Was Nebuchadnezzar thinking of the dream he had of a gigantic statue which he had seen towering above him, and got an idea? Well, maybe, but it was now twenty years later and I guess that if he wanted to make that statue of the dream he would have done it sooner.

I guess he was just wanting to produce a symbol of his power and his glory. Every human dictator has wanted a symbol. It is one of the signs of a dictatorship developing, a totalitarian state. I need only mention the swastika to give you an idea of the desire for a symbol that spells "power" that will cause people to fear. I believe that he was symbolising not necessarily himself nor even necessarily his gods – the chapter indicates it was not a god, it was a symbol of his power. It was the embodiment of the state.

Its purpose was not just to symbolise but also to unify and to bring all the empire together in a religious ceremony that would focus attention on his, Nebuchadnezzar's, power. So he sent throughout his empire for all the princes, the governors, the treasurers, the officials, and they all had to come. When they were gathered on the plain, probably three hundred thousand of them, he said, "Right, when the band plays, get down." Only one man was allowed to stand when the band played and that was Nebuchadnezzar.

The serious side of that situation is that this is the perfect picture of totalitarian regimes. Man is a religious animal and sooner or later, if a state is to have total control of a person, it must control his soul as well as his body. It must develop its own religion. There are two stages in which a nation does this. Stage number one is to have an established religion in which everybody has got to take part in the religion of the state. It is not so long since this applied in England, when if you were a Baptist you would be thrown into prison because you did not go to the established church. That is step number one.

Step number two is to make the state a religion and to say, "We will worship the state." So the state will develop its religious ceremonies, its hymns. We have seen this happen again and again. It happened in Roman imperialism where they used to set up a statue of Caesar and say, "Now bow down and say, 'Caesar is lord,'" and the only people who wouldn't do that were Jews and Christians – the Christians because they said "Jesus is Lord."

We have seen it in Nazi Germany in the 1930s. We saw it all develop, the religious ceremonies, the worship, the word "Heil". We have seen it in Russian Communism and Chinese Communism. We have seen it all develop – the symbolism, the religious ceremonies, the attempt to unify people in quasi-religious political dedications. This is what Nebuchadnezzar was doing. Therefore, he was saying: I don't care if you have your other gods; I don't care what religion you practise in private, but here in public you worship the state of Babylon and you bow down when the band plays.

Of course music, being such a moving thing and being so impressive in itself, can be used for evil as well as for good. We must always be careful to ask what kind of thing is happening when this music plays. What is it making us do? Is it making us healthier, more wholesome people, or is it driving us away from God? There is plenty of both kinds of music in our world today doing that. So the band played. Somebody once said to me, "When I hear a brass band, I'm ready to hit anybody or anything pretty hard!"

"So when the band plays, down you go" – imagine stirring,

military music, and the great statue shining in the plain, ninety feet up. The people had to get down on their faces, and that is totalitarianism. A substantial proportion of the human race may be under that kind of regime. It is frightening.

In that situation it looked as if nobody had any choice. Just to prove that Nebuchadnezzar thought he really was god he decided to have his own version of hell for the disobedient. He had a fiery furnace, which was his own private hell, and he said, "If you don't bow down and worship, then that's where you go." It had gone to the man's head and he thought he was a god. But out of the three hundred thousand people flat on that clay plain there were three still standing up. It takes courage to stand up when there are only three of you.

Do you ever feel you're alone in the office and in the shop? Do you ever feel that the pressures on you are too great? Next time you feel like that, just say, "Shadrach, Meshach, and Abednego," and see what happens. Nebuchadnezzar, standing himself, looked around, or rather others sneaked to peek, and some Chaldeans who should have been in the top cabinet ministry jobs, who had been very jealous of these Jewish boys who had got into the jobs before them, reported straight away. Maybe Nebuchadnezzar was not near enough to see the three, but those others had seen them and so they came and accused them.

Now let me just say a little about these three men. How very easy it would have been for them to get down. All they would have needed do would be to say something like this to themselves: "Well, everybody is doing it and I don't need to mean it. I can bow my head and I can pray to my God and no one will know. After all, we've got to live. We're in this situation and there are certain things you've got to do in order to live." Can't you see people being tempted to argue like that? After all, they were very few and what witness could they hope to make by being different?

We have heard all such arguments and we have used them on ourselves when we have been in a tight spot, to argue ourselves out of simple obedience. "We've just got to do that in our line of business," or, "just to get anywhere." "After all, I want to witness to them so I've got to be in among them, so I've got to compromise at some point." But these three men remembered one thing from the Word of God, "You must not make any image and bow down to it because God is jealous" – and that was enough to hold them. All the arguments for compromise you can put on one side of the balance, and you can put one text on the other side and the question is settled – and these three stood.

So they were accused by malicious enemies jealous of their position. The accusation was threefold – three charges of treason. "Nebuchadnezzar, they give no heed to your decree. Nebuchadnezzar, they give no service to your gods. Nebuchadnezzar, they give no worship to your image." You notice the key word in the three charges? "Your, your, your." To show their malice, they even went on to say, "Nebuchadnezzar, these are the men whom you appointed to have charge of Babylonian affairs." Your, your, your, you. In other words, it is a matter of personal pride. Nebuchadnezzar was cut where it hurts. His pride hurt badly and he was furious, raging with anger. *My* decree and they take no notice? *My* image and they won't bow down? *My* god and they won't worship. My, my, my.

Now it is amazing really how he spoke to them. He said, "I can't believe this of you." How subtle that was. You know, I thought you were my loyal friends. I thought we were getting on so well together. I can't believe this is true. How subtle! Then he said, "Look, I'm sure there's been a misunderstanding. You go right back there and when the band plays again, down you go. Mind you, if you don't...." Alas, Nebuchadnezzar couldn't shut his mouth at that point.

He had to go on and say something that clinched it for those three. He said, "If you don't, you go into the furnace and what can your God do about that?"

For Nebuchadnezzar to challenge their God was to make them determined to see it through. To say that about their God—it was a direct challenge not just to Shadrach, Meshach and Abednego, but to Almighty God. So those three men replied to the accusation calmly and quietly. I have never read braver words. Jesus said to disciples: "When you are before kings and governors, and you don't know what to say and you are being accused, don't worry about what to say. The Holy Spirit will give you the words."

The Holy Spirit gave these men words here. The first thing they said was, "Nebuchadnezzar" – now do you notice that? Not "king of kings" – that was his title. Not even, "Your majesty".

"O Nebuchadnezzar" – it was like saying, "O, John Smith." Do you see what they were saying? They were saying: you challenge God, Nebuchadnezzar, you are just a man. "O Nebuchadnezzar" – not even a title. Then, secondly, they were saying that there was no point in having any further discussion. Their minds were made up. There had been no misunderstanding. They knew what they were doing. They knew what they would face if they didn't do it. So there is no more discussion. "Nebuchadnezzar, we want to tell you this: that our God can deliver us from you or from anything at all, and he will deliver us." There was tremendous courage and faith.

Then came what I think is the most marvellous little phrase in the Old Testament almost, for sheer faith. Just three little words which take tremendous faith to say: "But if not...." If not, that would not alter anything. These weren't fair weather believers. These were not people who were godly because it paid. These were people who would do the right thing even if it didn't pay, and those are the kind of people that God wants.

"But if not..." – it makes no difference to our loyalty to God. Our faith in God and our loyalty to him are not dependent on his doing good for us or getting us out of trouble. It is because he is God that we trust him. "But if not, let it be known to you, Nebuchadnezzar, we are still not bowing down" – that is a tremendous statement. They would have understood the words, "The Lord is my helper and I will not fear what man does to me." That is what they were saying.

Nebuchadnezzar got so hot that when he held his hands out to the furnace it felt cool. He wanted the furnace as hot as himself. He was full of rage and so furious with these three, that they defied him and referred to him as a man, "Nebuchadnezzar", and just wouldn't accept his decree at all. Here were three men he could not control out of the whole empire, and it must have been maddening. So he said, "Heat that furnace seven times hotter." How would they do that? Well, normally they burnt wooden faggots in it, but as you know there is oil and bitumen in that area and they used it to cement their bricks together. Putting oil and bitumen into the furnace they would get a real blaze.

Don't people do silly things when they have lost their temper? It was the very worst thing to do – he should have cooled the fire down if he wanted to torture them. To heat it up would mean they would die very quickly, and it would also mean that his own best soldiers would be killed. How foolish this man looks. He is a bully, a coward, he has lost his temper, and he is doing very silly things.

Now let us come to the third part of the story: the miraculous deliverance. It would be a kind of beehive shaped lime kiln. You may have seen them, with an opening at the top and an opening at the side to bring the slag out.

So the prisoners would be bound and they would have to climb above this thing, with all the flames shooting up, to get them in, and that is when the soldiers died. But so much in a hurry was he that he didn't even bother to strip them. They tied them with ropes and they just threw them straight in. Now you may think that only one miracle took place but it wasn't just one, it was a series of them. Can you imagine their feelings as they fell down through the mouth of that kiln into that flaming furnace?

Nebuchadnezzar was later going to say of them, "They yielded their bodies to their God." That is quite a thing to say. Down they went. Nebuchadnezzar rushed around to the side to see them go. He would have to stoop and look in through the opening to see them burn. Now isn't this interesting? When the image was the centre of attention everyone was bowed down but Nebuchadnezzar was standing up. Now everybody is standing up but Nebuchadnezzar is bowing down, and there is somebody inside that furnace that he is bowing to though he doesn't know it. The drama of it! Isn't it tremendous?

What was happening inside the furnace? For one thing, their ropes were burning. The ropes that had bound them were just burning away until they dropped off, and not another thing was burnt. Clothes were not even scorched; hair – now that really goes first. If you have ever had a gas jet flame up in front of your face, your eyebrows and the front of your hair is gone. But not a hair was singed. When they came out, you couldn't even smell smoke on them, but that wasn't the only miracle.

When Nebuchadnezzar bowed down to look in he saw *four* men. Isaiah had said not long before, "When you go through the waters I'll be with you. When you go through the fire too" – and that's what was happening here. Now Nebuchadnezzar, in his own language and outlook, said:

it looks like a son of the gods. He couldn't say more than that. I have got to be honest and say that we can't press this too hard in any direction. It may have been an angel, as Nebuchadnezzar later said. It was an angel that was with Daniel in the lion's den. Or it may (and it could well have been) the Son of God himself with them. I don't think anybody can say dogmatically which it was. One thing is quite certain: somebody from heaven was in that furnace, a supernatural figure was the fourth.

So Nebuchadnezzar had to say, "God, their God, is the Most High God, higher than mine." He was so astonished that he called them out and they came out, and you know the rest of the story. He vindicated them totally. He praised their God and he praised them that they trusted in their God. He praised them for being disobedient; he praised them for yielding their bodies. Then he made a negative decree, which would protect them for the rest of their lives.

In typically despotic approach he said, "From now on, anybody who says a word against this God of theirs will do two things." I will tell you literally what he said because our English versions are often too nice. He said first, "If they say anything, "We'll rip their body into bits," and second, "We'll use their house to empty our closets in" – one of the common ways of degrading and causing someone to be disgusting in the eyes of the public. He said, "That's what we'll do if you speak against Shadrach, Meshach and Abednego."

You know, those poor people in that empire must have been brainwashed. They just didn't know what to do next. They couldn't please this man Nebuchadnezzar. "We all had to bow down to this one and now we can't say anything about that one." You can understand this is what happens when dictators begin to speak about religion. Poor old Nebuchadnezzar, he is still in charge, do you notice that? He is not bowing down to their God, he is lifting them up to his own level. What he should have done would be to prostrate himself before them as he had done to Daniel once. But instead he is saying: I'm going to lift you up to my level; I'll promote you; I'll give you a rise in salary. He didn't humble himself, he lifted them. That is why he was not yet converted – he still talked about their God not "mine". We will find in chapter four that he had to lose his sanity before he was converted. He had to be humbled to the dust, so he scrabbled around in the grass with claws like an animal, before he realised that God is God.

We now return to a phrase we noticed earlier: "But if not...." God delivered these three from the flames, but the simple fact is that there have been many more times when God has not delivered his people from the flames than the times when he did. It raises the very important question, which I want to tackle head on now, because I know it is important to you as it is to me: why does God deliver in certain situations and not in others? Why does God heal some people and not others? Is it arbitrary? Does he just pick us out with a pin? Or is it because we lack faith, those who are not delivered, and not healed, those who do burn to death as martyrs? Do they lack faith? What is the answer to this problem? It is a problem that I am being asked about almost every week.

Let us take the answer from God's Word. Why does God deliver in some situations and not in others? In the Victorian era or earlier, in addition to the Bible, a book that many Christian families read was *Foxe's Book of Martyrs*. Opening a copy, I saw a little coloured frontispiece of someone being burned at the stake for Christ. I turned the pages and found a picture of someone else being burned alive on an iron griddle, a saint who had gone through terrible things. He endured these tortures with such fortitude and perseverance that he was ordered to be fastened to a large gridiron with a slow fire under it. But his astonishing constancy and his serenity of countenance gave the spectators so exalted an idea of the dignity and truth of the Christian religion that many immediately became converts. He kept his sense of humour to the end because he said, "This side is broiled sufficient to be food for all who wish it to be done and good," at which they turned him over and boiled the other side. Then he cheerfully lifted up his eyes to heaven and with calmness yielded his spirit to the Almighty. This happened 10th August AD 258; Lawrence was his name.

I turn over again and find Jan Hus – the same thing. He was led to the suburbs of Constance to be burned alive. When he reached the place of execution he fell on his knees, sang several psalms, looked up to heaven and said, "Into thy hands, O Lord, do I commit my spirit." I turn more pages almost at random and find the martyrdom of William Flower. The faggots were piled around him and immediately he cried out, "O Son of God, have mercy on me." He repeated these words three times when the violence of smoke took away his speech. The lower parts of his body were consumed a considerable time before the others were much affected. At length however, the executioner finished his miseries by striking him a violent blow on the head.

Go to Oxford today and you will find a monument in the middle of the street where Latimer and Ridley were burned to death – where Latimer said to the young man Ridley to comfort him as the fires were lit, "Be of good comfort Mr Ridley and play the man. We shall this day light such a candle by God's grace in England as I trust shall never be put out." We turn more pages and here is the martyrdom of Archbishop Cranmer. Just before his death he signed a paper renouncing his convictions, but when it came to the point of his burning to death, he took the hand that had signed that recantation and he held it in the flames until it was burned away to nothing, and died trusting God – and so it goes on. Now why? Where is the God of Shadrach, Meshach and Abednego? I searched for the answer in the Bible and I found it not in the Old Testament but in the New. I found a passage in the New Testament where Shadrach, Meshach and Abednego are mentioned, but not by name. I found a passage in Hebrews 11 which says about the heroes of faith: "Time failing to list them all who by faith stopped the mouths of lions" – and that comes out of the book Daniel; and "quenched the power of raging fire" – and I believe that is referring to Shadrach, Meshach and Abednego. It says there that by faith these heroes escaped death, escaped the edge of the sword, put kingdoms to flight. Then, as I read on in that same paragraph, to my astonishment something hit me that has never hit me before. It says that by faith they escaped the edge of the sword and were killed by the sword. Astonishing! Faith to be killed by the sword? It went on: some were sawn asunder, stoned and wandered in deserts, mountains, in dens and caves of the earth. All these attested by faith. I realised more fully than ever before that you need faith to die as well as to be saved; that you need faith to be sick as well as to be well. I began to ask: "Which requires the greatest faith?" I could not answer that question. Faith that God will enable you to escape the edge of the sword, or faith to believe that God kills with the sword? Is this faith?

Then I went back to Shadrach, Meshach and Abednego, and they said, "He will deliver us from your hand," and then they said, "but if not...." Now that is a contradiction. Was their faith wavering? Then I saw something that came home with tremendous force. I went to a hospital to see a man aged about forty who was dying of cancer. He was only being kept alive with a drip of liquid food. He had a lovely wife and two little girls to leave behind. It was one of those holy moments when one just didn't have anything to say – I wanted to listen. This man said, "Either the Lord will take the cancer out of my body or he'll take me out of my body, and so he is going to cure me one way or the other." Now that requires tremendous faith. It is double faith. That is not just faith to be healed, it is faith to be ill. It is what Nebuchadnezzar said of Shadrach, Meshach, and Abednego: "They yielded their bodies." If you demand that God does one thing with your body and not another, you have not yielded your body. I believe it requires both kinds of faith. Shadrach, Meshach and Abednego yielded their bodies to God, not knowing whether God would glorify himself by delivering them from the flames or delivering them from their bodies. But he would deliver them, and they were quite sure of that.

Now I think that gives a bigger perspective on things. There are moments when God says to us, "I want you to have faith to be delivered in this way, by physical safety or health," and there are other times when he says, "I want you to be believing and trusting in me to deliver you this way." When I went back to Hebrews 11, I found that of those who were delivered from their enemies by death and by being killed with the sword, something was said of those people that was not said of the others. It was said of those people, "… of whom the world was not worthy." What an honour. God was saying of those who were killed with the sword that they were too good for the world to keep them. Isn't that remarkable? Too good for the world to keep them and so God took them.

I read on in Hebrews 11 and into Hebrews 12: "looking to Jesus, the author and finisher of our faith." Faith – and Jesus, at thirty-three, faced death. He knew what it was to have the struggle to want to be saved, and he said, "O God, if it's possible take this cup from me," and he had said, "All things are possible with God." But he had the battle and then he came through, and then he said, "Your will be done, not mine," and the emphasis is not on the word "will" but on the word "done".

This is not a resignation – "whatever will be will be" – it is resolution: whatever will be done, will be done. It is to believe that God can glorify himself and fulfil his plan and purpose in more ways than one. We say, "Lord you've got to deliver us this way," and God says, "I will glorify myself." So you come to the point with that great man of God, Job, who said, "Though he slay me, yet will I trust him." Faith!

These three had faith: "Let it be known to you, Nebuchadnezzar, that our God is able. But whether he does it or not, we trust him and we will not bow down to anything or anyone else."

4

IMPERIAL INSANITY
Read Daniel 4

A. MEANING OF A DREAM (1–27)
    1. Fate feared (1–18)
    2. Future foretold (19–27)
B. MADNESS OF A DICTATOR (28–37)
    1. Reign removed (28–33)
    2. Reason recovered (34–37)

Daniel chapter four is one of the most remarkable documents of human history for two reasons. First, it is a state document. We have very few such documents from the ancient world, and here is one of them preserved for us. It is a decree sent out by one of the most powerful emperors the world has ever known, to all the peoples within his empire. The second thing that makes it remarkable, and the most surprising thing of all, is that it is not a declaration of war, which such state documents often were – it is a declaration of peace and says, "Peace be multiplied to you."

The reason for this is that this document is a testimony. I do not know of a single other state document that is the testimony of an emperor, a king or a ruler. Here is a man who found God, and who wants the world to know, and he puts it in a state document which must be read in every corner of his empire, to all the peoples he has conquered. This man, who has conquered all those people is saying, "God has conquered me!" Oh, if one just heard some world ruler today issue a state document to the same effect!

Mind you, it took a lot of doing. God had to tackle this emperor three times before he won the battle. Do you notice each of those three times becomes more drastic, more fierce in experience than the preceding one? If a man rejects God once, when God speaks the second time it will be in a more drastic way. How wise you are, when you first hear the Word of God, to come! How wise to respond at the first touch of his Spirit. If you don't, he will have to speak harder next time and it will not be as comfortable.

Nebuchadnezzar was first spoken to by God in a nightmare, which caused him a deep disturbance of his feelings within. He was told the meaning of his dream, and was warned that it meant that his power would not last; that his empire would be replaced; that one day all human civilisation would collapse and be replaced by the kingdom of God. Did he listen? Was his heart changed? Was he converted? The answer is no. He simply promoted Daniel and bowed down before Daniel. So God had to speak more fiercely to Nebuchadnezzar.

Some twenty years later, God stepped into his life again, when Nebuchadnezzar, in his pride, caused there to be a state religion and a statue, and demanded that everybody bow down. As you know, three men were thrown into a fiery furnace, and Nebuchadnezzar thought he could send people to hell. The fiery furnace was his own private hell; he thought he was God. God spoke this second time by a miracle! But, believe me, when people see miracles, they do not believe in God. Don't kid yourself that that is all that is needed. Nebuchadnezzar had his own power over Shadrach, Meshach and Abednego neutralised by the power of God, and still Nebuchadnezzar didn't bow to God. It is true he issued a decree that no one must stop these three men believing in their God, which was a step forward, but still Nebuchadnezzar has not bowed the knee before God.

So God waited maybe another twelve years and then stepped into this man's life again, and this time in the most drastic way of all through a tragedy, a disaster. Sometimes a man who is at the top of his career, at the peak of his power, has to have a disaster overtake him before he will bow the knee to God. We read the tragic story of how Nebuchadnezzar became a man of God and when we get to heaven, we will meet him. Isn't that exciting? We are dealing with contemporary facts, with the here and now.

During the period between chapters three and four, Nebuchadnezzar, as he says, was at peace and enjoying prosperity; he was at rest and flourishing. He had conquered everything he wanted to conquer. The whole empire was under control, and money was pouring in from the taxes he imposed. He was at peace and prosperous. What did he do during that decade when he had peace and prosperity? The answer is that he decided to build the most magnificent capital the world had ever seen. This is what happens when nations are at peace and prosperous – they build themselves up, and this is what Nebuchadnezzar did.

If you were to go today to Baghdad, the capital of Iraq, and then cut due south across the flat alluvial plain of the Mesopotamian Basin, you would come to a vast area, miles across, of heaps of rubble and brick. You have come to Babylon. You can still pick your way around the broken bricks. Archaeologist after archaeologist has been to this place and uncovered some of the grandeur and magnificence of this city. I can hardly begin to describe it, but Nebuchadnezzar built it of brick. They had no stone in the middle of that plain. They had clay, and so they built it of bricks about fifteen inches square and three inches deep. On ten thousand of those bricks already uncovered, there is the name of Nebuchadnezzar inscribed in the middle, in a little kind of plaque of cuneiform writing: "I Nebuchadnezzar built this." With these bricks he built towers and walls. His own palace had a wall six miles long around it – far bigger than Buckingham Palace. He built magnificent gateways. There is one about the size of Tower Bridge—the Ishtar Gate. It was covered with the most beautiful blue glazed tiles depicting beasts. These beasts were an attempt to improve on the Creator's work. It was his pride that he thought he could make better beasts than God did, and so he made beasts with a snake's head, a lion's body and eagle's claws on its back legs.

He married a queen and she came from what is now Iran, Persia; Media. She lived up in the hills, and when she came to marry this man she missed the mountains. So with these bricks Nebuchadnezzar built her some huge, man-made mountains. You could see them for miles. The queen said that she missed the trees, and the forests of the mountains. Nebuchadnezzar said, "So do I. My favourite spot in the kingdom is Lebanon, and those lovely forests of Lebanon." (I am telling you now what he actually said; I'm not imagining this.) So together they planned a hanging garden, and they said, "On the top of these brick mountains, let's have trees and hanging plants, so that we've got mountains, forested mountains here, right in the middle of Babylon." So they built the Hanging Gardens, which were one of the Seven Wonders of the World. Tourists came from the whole empire to see the Hanging Gardens of Babylon. So they built this magnificent city, and everybody who came gasped. Sydney Opera House was nothing compared with this. They would look at the magnificent buildings, and Nebuchadnezzar would strut around. Of course, if you looked more closely in the back streets you would find poverty, beggars, rags and disease, but they were not the parts the tourists saw. The tourists came to the Ishtar Gate and walked down the Processional Way; they looked up to the right and saw the palace and the Hanging Gardens, and the great field surrounded by the palace wall in which Nebuchadnezzar kept wild animals as a private zoo; and away in the distance the Ziggurat, a temple to worship the stars. They saw all that and went away deeply impressed.

Now that was what was happening. So Nebuchadnezzar was at peace, and at rest, and you get the feel of this magnificent city. God loved Nebuchadnezzar enough to take away that rest. Thank God that he destroys a peace that is false. God looked down on that man, and he loved that man, and he couldn't leave him like that. God then had a third go at Nebuchadnezzar to try and get through to him. One night, Nebuchadnezzar went to bed and lay down on that huge, comfortable, superb bed but he couldn't sleep. When he did get to sleep, his brain dreamt. Suddenly he dreamed. You know the dream, having read about it in Daniel 4. This great big tree fell to the ground, just a stump, bound with bands of iron; and then there was a shoot coming from the stump again. He woke up in a cold sweat, and his thoughts were confused. You know, he could see this dream when he was awake, because it says it was not only a dream, it was a vision also, and that is something that happens when you are awake, and he saw this thing again. So it was with him vividly and he went on thinking about it.

Why did he not send for Daniel straight away? I have the feeling he didn't want to get the true interpretation. He sent for all those silly wise men – excuse the phrase, but that's what they were. His silly wise men tried hard, and they couldn't tell him what it meant. I would have thought that anybody with his head screwed on straight could have told Nebuchadnezzar the meaning of that dream in its basic essentials, for this reason. Archaeologists have dug up a clay tablet on which is written something that Nebuchadnezzar said. These are the words on that clay tablet: "My empire," says Nebuchadnezzar, "is like a spreading tree, growing over the world." He had said it in one of his public speeches and the scribe had written it down in the clay. We have it in a museum today. He had said he was a spreading tree, and the wise men couldn't tell him what it meant. Maybe they didn't want to, for fear he would chop them down. At any rate, he couldn't get the truth out of them, but there was a fear in his heart. I think Nebuchadnezzar knew the basic meaning. He knew that it was a threat to him and his reign. He just knew that, so he didn't want Daniel telling him so.

Finally, he sent for Daniel and said, "Daniel, let's not beat about the bush. The spirit of the holy gods is in you." Now that was the nearest he could get to saying, "You're filled with the Holy Spirit." That's how a pagan would talk but he was recognising that Daniel was full of the Spirit, and therefore he was able to say, "Daniel, because you're full of the Spirit, mysteries are no problem to you." That was a double tribute to this man. I will tell you this, when the world is puzzled and perplexed, when they can't get an answer to the question, they will come to a Spirit-filled man of God because they believe he will have the answer. "So, Daniel, tell me the truth," and he told him the dream.

The meaning of the dream is very clear. Daniel says, "The meaning is: the tree is you, and you should know that. Your leaves have spread out; your branches have spread out; the animals and the birds represent the nations that have come." This is a favourite picture in the Bible. Jesus once said, "The kingdom of heaven is like a mustard seed which grows into a great tree; and the birds of the air come and lodge in the branches" – here is a familiar picture of the nations coming into the kingdom of God, and that bit of it is straightforward. Then says Daniel: "The angels are going to chop you right down and rob you of the entire kingdom. The whole lot will go and you're going to lose everything. You're even going to go lower than a man who's got nothing; you're going to go down and down. For seven years, you will live like an animal." Then Daniel says, "But there's something more. I noticed that the stump was bound." Do you know why they bound stumps with bands of iron and brass in the ancient days? It was to stop the stump from splitting and rotting, in the hope that it would grow again. So Daniel says, "There is hope. I can see that the stump is bound and held and remains. It's not uprooted, and after seven years, it'll grow again." Now that is the dream, and that is its meaning.

I want to point out two things: the concern of Daniel before he gave the dream's interpretation, and his counsel after he had done so. He did not just pass on the message. He was not one of these heartless people who can announce news with no feelings, no concern for those to whom the bad news is announced. Daniel, before he could tell the news, was struck with horror. This man felt for the person he has got to say it to. We have got to tell our world that they are going to hell; we have got to tell them that the judgment of God is coming, but we must be silent first and concerned about it before we do. Otherwise we have got no feeling for people. It should never be easy for a preacher to preach on hell or judgment. Daniel couldn't bring himself to preach that sermon, and he sat there aghast at the meaning. Nebuchadnezzar saw his difficulty and said, "Don't be afraid. I'm not going to do anything to you. Just tell me the truth. You know, don't you? I can see it on your face. You won't tell me. Tell me." Daniel's concern was for Nebuchadnezzar, wicked tyrant though he was; cruel dictator though he was, and Daniel nevertheless said, "I wish what I've got to tell you I could say about your enemies and not you." What a heart this man has! Not just a head to understand mysteries, but a heart to feel for people when the judgment of God is being announced.

Therefore, not only did he show concern before he told him the dream, he gave him counsel afterwards. God doesn't judge people for no reason at all; he doesn't knock a ruler down because he wants to, picking him out with a pin. God operates on moral principles, and he would never do this to a man unless that person deserved it. God would not have told Nebuchadnezzar he was going to cut him down like that unless there was something wrong. If God was going to cut Nebuchadnezzar down out of sheer judgment and had no mercy for him, he wouldn't have warned him beforehand.

When God warns us that he is going to do something, it is his mercy giving us a chance – because the past is fixed, but the future is still flexible and can be changed. Praise God for his warnings! God warned in the days of Noah, and he waited 120 years, and then another week, before he sent the rain. That was mercy as well as judgment. You find that the Bible is full of warnings of the end of the world and the judgment to come. We have no excuse for not getting ready. God, in his mercy, tells us beforehand that he is going to do it – to see how we react, for the future can be changed. That is the glorious possibility.

So Daniel is giving Nebuchadnezzar hope. God was trying to get through to this king. He needed to turn away from his sins. What about those poor people in the city? Why not spend some money on them? He should leave his past, change, and live right. At least then he might be able to stay this judgment that is coming; he might get a period of peace. Daniel is pleading for this man. If ever we announce judgment and wrath to other people, it must be with concern beforehand and counsel afterwards. That is the framework to preach the judgment of God.

Well, that is the first part of the story. I must now turn to the very sad sequel. Twelve months passed. What did Nebuchadnezzar do in that year? Did he stop spending money on his palace and his garden and his city? Did he go down to the streets and see what needs there were among the poor? Did he begin to lift the condition of his people? No, he very quickly forgot the dream and the fear it had caused; his conscience was lulled and his fears faded. The man went right back to his proud building programme.

The fact is that Nebuchadnezzar still was not changed in his heart. Time is the best test of whether a man is really sorry. Time is the best test of real repentance. What is he like a year later? That is the test, and by that test, Nebuchadnezzar is the same old sinner. We see it, as twelve months later we find him walking on those walls, which were wide enough to drive three chariots abreast along the top. The walls stretch along, around the field where the beasts were kept in the private zoo. As Nebuchadnezzar walked along that wall, and looked over the vast city as far as the eye could see, and saw the man-made mountains, he said, "Is not this great Babylon, which I have built by my power for my glory?"

Do you know what he's saying? It was similar to saying part of the Lord's Prayer, but changing a word, like this: "*mine* is the kingdom and the power and the glory". He was talking to himself; he probably felt that was the most intelligent conversation he ever had, and that he was the only person who would appreciate the greatness that he was talking about. So he was talking aloud to himself. "Is not this great Babylon which *I* have built by *my* mighty power as a royal residence and for the glory of *my* majesty?" This was pride, with a capital "I" in the middle.

As he strutted around the great city, it was impressive; it was great; it was enough to make any man's heart burst with pride; but God was listening to the conversation and wanted to join in. A voice from heaven came. God had waited twelve months for this man to humble himself, and the simple truth is that if we do not humble ourselves before Almighty God, then he will humble us. We will be humble one way or the other—how much better to be humble the easy way and not the hard way.

The voice from heaven told Nebuchadnezzar that the Most High rules the kingdom of men and gives it to whom he will. When Nebuchadnezzar came back into his palace he was on all fours, snarling, and scrabbling into the palace, and his staff stared. They realised the man was mad. They drove him out into that palace garden, into his own private zoo, into what was called the field. They kept him there and let him roam around until his nails were long and sharp, scrabbling the grass; and he lived on grass for seven years. His hair grew longer and longer, always a disgrace for a man. He just became a beast – dirty, matted, with the rags of his royal robes clinging to him – and that was Nebuchadnezzar. This happened – this is not just fiction, it is something that really occurred.

It is strange that people today are so concerned to try to prove that we have come up from the animals. We are so worried about it, partly because if we could prove evolution, we could try then to go on to prove that it all happened by chance, and we have ruled God out. But we should be concerned lest God turn us into animals, not whether we have come up from there, but whether we are going to go down to there. That is what happened to Nebuchadnezzar, and it can happen to any human being. This is what the Bible means by "perished". It means that a man loses his humanity. It gives us a glimpse of what hell really will be like – can you imagine it? People who used to be human beings with human feelings, now just animals because the simple fact is that when a man is cut off from God he does become a beast. Scripture does not support the idea that man once was a beast, but it does support the truth that he can become a beast.

Nebuchadnezzar stands as an example to all proud people, that God can bring the proud down to the dust from which he made us. It is a rare form of madness, but not unknown. I was reading a documented case of such a malady in 1946 in Britain where somebody suffered from lycanthropy, as it is called, in which a person literally behaves like an animal. In this case, in the hospital to which they were sent, they lived on the grass of the lawns of the hospital, and just behaved like an animal.

For seven years that went on, and then, one day, Nebuchadnezzar's sanity returned. I am going to use my imagination a little here and speculate. As he scrabbled about on all fours, searching for grass and maggots and what have you, did he come to one of the pools in the palace garden?

Do you think he had bent down to take a drink, and suddenly saw two eyes looking at him and recognised them in the reflection? Do you think he saw also the reflection in the pool of the clouds and sky? Something an animal never does is to lift its head to heaven. An animal's attention is earthbound. Have you ever watched animals in a field? Have you ever watched them looking at the stars and studying the clouds? No, it is only man who walks upright on the earth and looks up to heaven. From the reflection in the pool he saw those two eyes; he saw himself, and a gleam of recognition came into that beast-like face; and he saw the clouds, and he lifted his eyes to heaven, and sanity returned. Isn't that tremendous? One just wants to say to the whole human race today: lift your eyes to heaven, and we'll have a sane world again. As long as you are earthbound and look at the chaos and the tragedy of our world around us, it is enough to drive you insane. For it is insane, the things we do to each other. Have you watched the scenes from war? Isn't it insane? Let's lift our eyes to heaven and let sanity return.

Nebuchadnezzar looked up for the first time in seven years and reason came back. He knew who he was. This is a symbol of our whole human race: we don't know who we are until we lift our eyes to heaven. He praised and honoured and blessed God. He holds a private prayer meeting! The palace staff come out and see Nebuchadnezzar praising God – "Bless you, God!" I daresay there were some of the palace staff who said his madness had taken a new turn. Today when you are praising God outside church, some people say: "It's religious mania." I have no doubt they said of Nebuchadnezzar, "He's got even worse, poor chap, you know it's all due to that breakdown he had" – and they would have said that till the end of his days. But don't you believe it! He was never so sane in his life as the day he recovered. He realised that he had not only been insane for seven years, he had been insane for his whole life. He saw how foolish it all was now. He said, "O God, you're God; you're the King; you're eternal." He declared God's sovereignty, greatness and goodness. He thanked the Lord. Now he could see clearly who was God.

It is a great account and it has a happy ending. The palace was so thrilled to have him back – his courtiers and his staff. I have no doubt that Daniel had managed to hold the thing together and had told them that he would recover. For seven years, Daniel must have carried the brunt of this, and persuaded them to hold on and to wait. Now it had come true, and Nebuchadnezzar was back in the palace. They put his robes on, cut his hair, shaved him, washed him, and sat him on the throne. Nebuchadnezzar was given back his glory and his kingdom. God destroyed nothing that Nebuchadnezzar had built, because now he could be trusted with power. Never again would he abuse it. Never again would he think he was God. He would realise that he was emperor of Babylon by the grace of God, and so Nebuchadnezzar was saved.

Evidently, pride goes before a fall, but I would say the moral is this: *the way up is down*. I want to apply this story to the world's rulers first. Mussolini once said, "I recognise no sovereignty outside my own will." Hitler said the same; Stalin said the same; Mao Tse Tung said the same – in their own words. We want to say most solemnly that God brings all these dictators down to the level of the beast. He will not take that kind of challenge.

Nebuchadnezzar did it in Babylon, the very place where, centuries earlier, the Tower of Babel had been built up as a challenge to heaven. God will always accept that challenge. He deals with it; the mills of God grind slowly, but they grind exceeding small. That great Scottish Christian Andrew Melville said to King James VI of Scotland, "Thou weak servant! There are two kingdoms in Scotland and two kings: King James and King Jesus, of whom James is neither head nor lord, but subject." What a statement! What courage to say that.

One would like to hear a British political party leader say, "God will decide the next election. The British government is in God's gift, and he can give it to whomever he pleases." Let all the parties in England pray that God will do *his* will. Let's forget opinion polls and seek God's government. Oh, for a state document like this! Many years ago, Queen Wilhelmina of the Netherlands said, "By the grace of God, and in dependence upon him, I have reigned for fifty-eight years." The real people who reign in England are not the royal family. We have long since left that behind. Let's be realistic in our prayers and in our thinking.

At one election in the twentieth century there were at that time five declared atheists in the cabinet of our British government as ministers of state. When the next election came there were hundreds of Christians throughout the UK praying for one thing: that God would give us a cabinet without any atheists on it. There was a surprise swing in that election which was explained on all sorts of other grounds, but the result was that there was not one declared atheist in the next cabinet. We can start praying now for the next General Election.

Lest we point this chapter in the wrong direction, and point it all to the rulers of the world – this chapter is relevant to every person reading this. For you don't need Babylon, you just need a nice garden, and you can do the same thing. "Is not this *my* garden, which I've spent so much time and money on, and is so beautiful, and the neighbours all admire it? Is not this *my* house?" You can be houseproud with just one room. You can say, "Is not this *mine*, which I have built, which I'm responsible for?" You can do it with your children. "Are not these *my* children, to whom I have given this education – *my* upbringing? Oh, I am so proud!" The

Lord gave you your house and your garden and your children. It is spelling "pride" with a capital "I" in the middle that challenges God, and you can do it in one room; you can do it with a window box. We need to remember that God can't stand human pride and he can bring *us* low too.

Many years ago there was a famous preacher in the north of England called Dr W. L. Watkinson. He went to preach in Lancashire, and was invited to stay the day with a self-made Lancashire cotton mill owner – the kind of man who had got plenty of brass, and was building himself up. He had got a lovely stone house in the Pennines, and an estate next to the big mill that he had built. All through lunch he was telling Dr Watkinson how he had built up the mill with his own efforts, and how it was a glory to his family name, and all the rest.

After lunch they went for a walk through the estate. The man had just planted a row of birch trees. He said to Dr Watkinson, "Look at those birches. I've planted them for my posterity." Dr Watkinson said, "They might be more use on your posterior." He was a blunt northern preacher, and he was just saying to that Lancashire mill owner: "Nebuchadnezzar!" Next time you have got this heart of pride – "Is not this which I did, which I built up for my strength, my glory?" instead of thanking God for the sheer delight of doing a good job, and for the gifts that made it possible – just remind yourself about Nebuchadnezzar.

Finally, consider this contrast: Nebuchadnezzar, thinking he was God because he had a vast empire; and Jesus, knowing that the Father had given all things into his hands, taking a towel and washing the feet of the disciples.

5

WRITING ON THE WALL
Read Daniel 5

A. BELSHAZZAR'S FEAST (1–9)
  1. Sacrilegious (1–4)
  2. Supernatural (5–9)
B. BELSHAZZAR'S FOLLY (10–23)
  1. Warned (10–21)
  2. Wilful (22–23)
C. BELSHAZZAR'S FATE (24–31)
  1. Foretold (24–28)
  2. Fulfilled (29–31)

The message of Daniel chapter 5 is very simple: God has no grandsons. Godliness cannot be inherited from generation to generation, or as we put it more crudely in the north of England, "Muck to muck in three generations." You may have grandchildren who have no time for God. It does not follow that if your grandfather knew and loved the Creator of heaven and earth that you will too.

Every generation needs to discover for itself the power of God, and therefore any generation can lose the godliness of its forebears. This is what happened to Nebuchadnezzar's grandson Belshazzar. In one night he lost everything that his grandfather had built up, and he did it through a single act of defiance against God. He did it for just one reason: he got the worse for drink. That may be a real lesson that we will get out of this chapter, but first a bit of history.

Until comparatively recently, people used to say that Daniel was fiction. There are still many scholars who say that it is a lot of stories that have been made up with little bits of history pushed in, but a lot of inaccuracies. For example, of this very chapter they said two things. They said first, "The name of Belshazzar has never been found anywhere outside the Bible, so how do we know he even existed?" The second thing they stated was that all the records of secular history that had been discovered said that the last emperor of Babylon was a man called Nabonidus, not Belshazzar. So they ridiculed Daniel and said, "Can't be true."

Now we are beginning to learn again that you can't mock God and that you can't laugh at God's Word. For one thing, as late as 1958 or 1960, the text was published of a cylinder, which you can see in a museum in Florence today, and there, written bold as brass, is the word "Belshazzar". The name has been found, and we realise the sceptical scholars were trying to prove something that was wrong. The other matter that has come to light requires a very quick history lesson. Nebuchadnezzar died after a reign of forty-three years. He had one son called Evil – what a name to give your boy! Of course, it didn't mean that then, it only means that in English now. But Evil only survived two years and was then assassinated by his brother-in-law, a man called Neriglissar. This brother-in-law then took the throne. He was therefore the son-in-law of Nebuchadnezzar, having married Nebuchadnezzar's daughter. He managed to survive four years before he died. His son then came to the throne and only survived nine months and then he was beaten to death by a gang of conspirators; among the conspirators was a man called Nabonidus, who thus took the throne for the last reign of the empire of Babylon. What a story, isn't it? What a kingdom!

Nabonidus married Nebuchadnezzar's daughter, the widow of Neriglissar, but it does mean that the last king's son, whom he called Belshazzar, was in the royal line, though he himself, Nabonidus, was not. Therefore, Belshazzar had more of Nebuchadnezzar's blood in him than his father had. And so, since Nabonidus was frequently going away around the empire, absent on business, he made his son, Belshazzar, co-regent, the second ruler of the kingdom.

When this story opens, Nabonidus is not only away, he is in exile because he has been defeated in battle by Cyrus; and so he is away in Arabia. His son, the co-regent, the second ruler of the kingdom, is holding the empire together while his father is away in exile – which explains why he offered Daniel the position of third ruler in the kingdom. Until this was all discovered, people said "Why third ruler?" Now it all makes sense, and the whole thing clicks into place. Those who have laughed at the accuracy of Daniel are not smiling now – they have had to think again!

This is the kind of thing that happens over and over again

with people who say the Bible is full of contradictions and inaccuracies. It simply means we are ignorant of the whole picture, and when we know more we find it fits beautifully. So we approach Daniel chapter 5 with tremendous confidence. God is a God of truth and this is his Word and therefore this is truth, and not just fictional truth or moral truth, but historical truth. God would not want to lie to us. God would not want to mislead us. With God it is the truth, the whole truth and nothing but the truth!

Belshazzar's feast is a night in the month of October in the year 539 BC and Belshazzar is a playboy prince. He had a huge banqueting hall – it has been discovered by archaeologists. It is half the size of a football pitch. The walls are white plaster, and opposite the king's platform in that hall there is a niche, which would be used for the largest candelabra – the lampstand, the candlestick that would throw light primarily on the king, but a lesser light along to the rest of the diners.

Presumably, it was in that very alcove, above that candelabra, opposite the king, on the white plaster, that a finger began to write. This is quite a feast, a thousand people in that hall, and their wives and their concubines; it is going to be quite a do! It is ladies' night at Belshazzar's court, and furthermore the wine is flowing freely. They are going to have a good time and that is the background to the party that went badly wrong.

Do you know what happens when you get a bit of drink inside you? Your inhibitions go. The things that deep down you have wanted to do, you begin to do. Thank God for inhibitions! We live in a day when inhibitions are supposed to be bad things; when you are supposed to be all tied up in knots if you have inhibitions. "Get rid of your oppressions, be yourself, express yourself, and do your own thing" – but that's a very dangerous thing to do because, as Paul discovered, "In me, that is in my flesh, dwells no good thing," and if I am going to let that out, things are going to go wrong.

Frankly, that is a good reason for not getting drunk, because many people have done things when they are a bit tipsy that later they have regretted in their sober moments. The inhibitions go down. You begin to do things for kicks. When I joined the RAF, a senior chaplain who taught me the ropes told me about "mess nights" in the officers' mess. He said, "You should go for the dinner, chat afterwards, but quietly slip out of the door at 9.15 p.m. They will appreciate it as chaplain, if you're out of the way after that." He added, "You will maintain your standards." I discovered what he meant very quickly. This is what was happening here – "mess night", and I think that word "mess" is a very appropriate word in the circumstances! So they began to get a bit tight, and Belshazzar began to want to do naughty things, and to want to do bold and brash things that would give the thrill of shocking people; that is what happens when you get a bit drunk.

Belshazzar remembered something. As he talked, and as he looked at the cups he was drinking from, he remembered an incident that probably happened when he was a boy, wandering around the palace of Babylon and had gone into a storeroom and seen some magnificent gold and silver cups. He would have asked, "What are these? Why are they never brought out? Why are they never used?"

Somebody then would have told him, "Your grandfather brought those away from Jerusalem. They are holy vessels. They belong to the God of Israel."

"Well, they are loot, booty. Why don't we bring them out and use them?"

The boy must have been told, "Your grandfather forbade us ever to use those for any purpose, because your grandfather came to believe in the Most High God. So we don't touch them. We keep them in the cupboard."

On the night when Belshazzar got a bit tipsy he thought, "I'm just going to do something that my grandfather would have disapproved of." Can't you see it all coming up in his heart? "Send for those vessels. We're going to toast our gods out of the vessels of this Most High God of Jerusalem."

He was doing it for kicks – that is why most people do this kind of thing. There is a certain thrill about being blasphemous, about a little bit of sacrilege. We see that on some satirical television shows in the modern era. Like many another person, Belshazzar was dabbling in something that he did not realise had consequences. He didn't realise that something supernatural might happen.

Belshazzar, drinking, lifted his eyes as he lifted his cup, and the cup fell from his hands. For, as he lifted his eyes, he saw on the far wall the supernatural response to his act of sacrilege: fingers writing on the wall. Can you imagine it? Supposing you saw that happen right now on a wall? How would you feel? I think your blood would run cold. Your heart would stop, and I will tell you this: conscience doth make cowards of us all. If you have got anything on your conscience you would feel far worse than the others.

This man Belshazzar realised that he had pushed God beyond the limit of patience – the same God who had sent his grandfather mad. Belshazzar went utterly to pieces. We are told that his face went white as the wall, his legs shook, he trembled. He joined the Quakers in a minute. That is the origin of that name, by the way. I am using it quite seriously. They trembled before Almighty God, and so people called them "the Quakers". Have you ever quaked before God? Many men of God have done. This is what Belshazzar did: he shook, he shouted – and the women screamed and the men jumped up. They didn't know whether to leave or what.

Belshazzar said, "Bring somebody who can tell me what

that means. Send for the wise men" – and they all came. Can you see the place in an uproar? The party went terribly wrong. This party was an extraordinary thing. While it was being held, the Persians had invaded the country and were even then at the gates of Babylon, yet this playboy prince does not care. He thinks the walls of Babylon will keep them out. His father is away in exile after being defeated by Cyrus, and yet this prince can hold this kind of an orgy. What a man! Just a young man at the time, too – perhaps that is why he did it.

Now the whole party has gone sour and they are trembling and shouting and screaming. They are staring. The fingers have disappeared, but the words are still there: Mene, Mene, Tekel, Parsin. What does that mean? The wise men came and shook their heads. He bribed them. He offered them everything. He said, "Look, a new suit; purple. No, you can't tell me? Then, third ruler in the kingdom; can you tell me now?" Trying to get something out of them; it's a pathetic scene. The reason they could not read the message is very simple: they didn't know who had sent it, and so it made no sense. Some scholars have said that it would have been consonants without vowels and that was why they couldn't read it; maybe it was in Chaldean, or what was to become Aramaic. We don't know exactly how it was written, and this is conjecture. I believe that they couldn't read it because it was all verbs, with no subjects and no objects. Suppose, for example, you got a telegram which said, "Called, cancelled, coming." Now if you knew who had sent it, you would be able to make sense of the telegram. You would say, "Ah, that's my business partner. He was going to call on another businessman to arrange a contract, but clearly it's been cancelled, so he's coming to see me again." Right, now "Called, cancelled, coming" makes sense because you know the person who sent it, and you know the situation behind it.

But this simply said four verbs, or three verbs, one repeated – and that is all it said.

The wise men did not know the God who had sent the message, so how could they tell what it meant? It is the same with the Bible. It is a book filled with messages from God, but if you don't know the one who sent them, you won't be able to make any sense of it for yourself. You will read it – it will be dull, boring, perplexing, but when you know the person who sent it, then it makes sense. So these wise men did not know the God who sent the message and so they could not understand it. Then a woman came to the rescue— the queen mother. I believe it was Nebuchadnezzar's widow, because her first words are identical to Nebuchadnezzar's words about Daniel.

The queen mother, hearing uproar, comes striding in and sees this descendant, this grandson of her king, in a disgraceful state. She says, "Pull yourself together. There is a man in your kingdom who can tell you what that means." No retirement for servants of God, you know – because Daniel would be about eighty-six when this happened. Maybe he thought he was going to be able to ease up, I don't know. I don't think he was that kind of chap. He realised there is no discharge in this war. God never enables you to retire at sixty-five, and God recalled Daniel at eighty-six to bring his word to this situation, as later God was going to bring Daniel to the lions' den at ninety-three. If you are old yourself, never believe that God can't use you any more. He can go on using you until you step into his presence – just to say a word for him at the right time. Maybe sometimes older people go through the severest test of their faith in their last years, but when they come through, like Daniel, isn't it tremendous? People talk of it for a long time.

So Daniel comes out of retirement, and he steps into this scene. Can you see it? Venerable, aged, calm, collected, into this chaos of Belshazzar's feast. Daniel doesn't tell Belshazzar what the writing means first, he preaches a sermon on Belshazzar's utter folly. He says it first because he knows he wouldn't listen afterwards, so he leads up to it and he says, "Belshazzar, you fool! Can you see how utterly silly you've been? First of all, because Belshazzar, you've been warned. Haven't you heard about your grandfather when he defied this God? Didn't you hear how he became mad and was an animal in the field in his own private zoo? Didn't you ever hear that?" Of course he knew that! Daniel says to Belshazzar, "You knew."

Now before you condemn Belshazzar for this foolishness, just think about how widespread folly is. Consider smoking – every packet of tobacco carries a government health warning. Doesn't that habit strike you as madness? Think about people playing with drugs – they should know that is slow suicide! And we can think of many other examples. Daniel says, "Belshazzar, you knew!" – but the folly of human nature is in every one of us: many know perfectly well what foolish things lead to, but they do them anyway. This is the folly of every man, not just Belshazzar.

"Belshazzar, you knew what happens, and yet, even though you were warned, you wilfully set yourself against this God and lifted yourself up in pride. You turned from the true God to false gods; from a living God to dead ones who cannot even see or hear or know anything." That is what the Bible thinks of other religions – gods who can't see, and who can't hear, and who don't know anything. It is a terrible indictment of Belshazzar, but Daniel is saying something that we need to say to ourselves and everyone. If you think you can get away with it, if you think you won't get caught, if you think you won't pay the bill, then just say to yourself: "Belshazzar – he thought just like that."

Now Daniel turns to Belshazzar's fate. He turns to the

message, and from his interpretation it is clear that it is already too late for Belshazzar to do anything about it. With Nebuchadnezzar he had twelve months after the warning to get right with God. We know he didn't and God had to drive him mad before he became sane, but with Belshazzar, his grandson, he didn't even get twelve hours before it came true, because a son who has had such warning, who has had such an example within his own family circle, has no excuse for going the same way himself. Therefore the message is one of unrelieved doom and tragedy. What is it? Daniel reads off the verbs, and then he supplies to each verb a subject and an object and another verb. He knows the God who wrote it, and therefore he can supply the full sentence from the telegram that God has sent.

The telegram reads, "Numbered, numbered, weighed, divided", but that makes no sense to anybody except a man of God. The man of God says, "I'll tell you what it means – "numbered", that is a verb, and the subject is "God", and the object is "days"; and the second verb is "finished".

"God has numbered your days and you're finished." The Psalmist says, "So teach us to number our days that we may apply to ourselves a heart of wisdom." The tragedy is we never do number our days; we always go on living as if we are here forever. When did you last number your days?

You could do that right now. Let us say that our day begins at six o'clock in the morning and ends at six o'clock at night, if that is our life. At what time of the day are you living right now? Have you asked yourself that question? Oh, teach us to number our days, because even if we don't number them, God does. What time of day is it for you? If you are young, it seems as if the day is stretching out ahead. It seemed to be stretching out for Belshazzar, but: "God has numbered your days and you're finished."

The second verb is "weighed". "God has weighed you,

Belshazzar, in his scales, and you are too light. You are lacking; you are not big enough a man for the job; you have been weighed in the balance and found wanting; you have been given the power of an empire, and you are frittering it away as a playboy."

"Weighed" – God is going to weigh every life in his scales.

Parsin, or the singular form of the plural verb *peres*, means "divided", but both words are like the word "Persian". From this pun, Daniel caught the clue from God: "God has divided your kingdom and is going to give it to the Medes and the Persians – going to split it up. This great empire will never be as big again – and that is the message, Belshazzar."

Why didn't God write all that out on the wall clearly? Why did he put it in a mysterious way? You get the same question when people ask, "Why should God give a message to a fellowship in tongues when people can't understand it, and somebody has to come in and interpret it?"

Same question: God sometimes does it this way to draw attention to his Word; to focus people on what he is saying even before they understand it, so that he may then co-operate with men in interpreting this, in giving a sense that this word is supernatural, direct. That was what he was doing. This was a written message in tongues, if you like, on the wall, and it needed the gift of interpretation. The attention it drew! How they concentrated on what Daniel said by way of interpretation.

The tragedy is that instead of asking whether anything could be done to avoid that, Belshazzar said, "Daniel, thank you very much. Come here, I've got a medal for you." Can you credit a man doing that? "Fetch a purple robe; you are third ruler from now on, Daniel. Great; that was really clever." The man must have been nearly as insane as his grandfather became if he could get a message from God like that, and then react in that way, isn't it astonishing?

Daniel accepted the gifts even though he had said, "Keep your gifts, give them to someone else" – because, frankly, they were worthless. He saw the king was past argument. What was the point in becoming the third ruler of a kingdom that was to fall that night? It was a worthless honour, and all the honours the world gives are worthless in the long run. I remember watching Churchill's funeral and seeing the medals and insignia of the honours he had received, lying on a cushion on top of his coffin, and I thought, "Poor man; you've had to leave them behind." The reason why honours of men are valueless in the long run is that the kingdoms of men disappear, and all that man does goes.

"Belshazzar, the enemy is not only at the gates of your city as you feast – already the enemy is inside the city." They were. We have three other sources from outside the Bible recording in writing what happened that night, confirming to the letter the last part of this chapter.

The troops of Darius were gathered outside the city, though that is probably a title rather than a name; and they were gathered outside the city, up against the walls that reached seventy-five feet or so up into the sky, with towers a hundred feet up. So confident were the Babylonians that their watchmen were drunk. Everybody was celebrating that night, and they laughed at the enemy at the gates. "You may have taken the rest of the empire, but you'll never get into this city. We can stand a siege of five years; you'll never do it." But that night the enemy got in. Do you know how they got in? They couldn't go over the walls, so they came under them. Flowing right through the middle of ancient Babylon was a great river, the River Euphrates, and the walls had to jump the river. They did, but the walls went to the level of the water. So what did the enemy do? He dug a channel from the river north of the city to a swamp at a lower level, and he drained off the River Euphrates into the swamp. When the water went down to four feet, he ordered his troops in from the north and the south along the riverbed, and they waded under the walls of Babylon.

While Belshazzar was putting the robe of purple on Daniel, the last official act of this empire was to honour a man of God – what irony of history there is here! While Belshazzar was doing that, the enemy was inside the walls, climbing out of the river. A few hours later, they burst into that very hall and they slew Belshazzar. See him now, the playboy prince lying in a pool of wine and blood, the golden and silver vessels of Jerusalem scattered on the floor around him; and his dead, non-seeing eyes staring up at that niche on the opposite wall: "Mene, mene, tekel, parsin."

A sixty-two year old king took Babylon that night. I am telling you fact, not fiction. It had been foretold by Daniel in Daniel chapter 2; it had been foretold by Isaiah: it had been foretold by Jeremiah. Whatever God says through his prophets will come to pass; it must happen. The greatest empire of the ancient world, Babylon, fell in a night, because its emperor got drunk. That is the kind of end to which human ambition comes. Babylon itself is a picture of the final days of human civilisation, for you read Revelation chapters seventeen, eighteen, and nineteen—the fall of modern Babylon, it's there.

The finger of God writes over everyone: you've been weighed in the balance, and you're not good enough. It doesn't mention in Daniel 5 what is in the other pan of the scales of God. When God puts you on this side of the balance, what does he put on the other side? Have you ever asked yourself that question? He puts the Lord Jesus Christ on the other side – that is who you are weighed against.

As I read Daniel 5, I thought of another occasion when the finger of God wrote. Can you think of another occasion when the finger of God wrote in the Bible? It was when a group of religious men dragged a half-naked woman into the presence of Jesus and said, "Stone her, stone her! We found her committing adultery," which means they had also found the man, but they had let him go. He was one of their sex, so they had let him off in spite of the Law of Moses. Jesus saw the whole malice and injustice of their attitude and it says: "Jesus stooped and, with his finger, wrote in the dust."

What did he write? Did he write, "Mene, mene, tekel, parsin?" They would have understood it if he did; but, you know, it was the finger of God writing, and as they watched that finger write, it says they left; beginning with the eldest, one by one they slunk away, because they knew they were wanting; lacking in God's sight; that Jesus was weighing them up, and they didn't pass. Finally, he was left alone with the woman, and he weighed her up too. He said, "Neither do I condemn you. Go and sin no more."

When you stand before God, and you are in the balances with Christ, do you know what I want to see written by God's finger on the wall? "There is now therefore no condemnation to them that are in Christ Jesus" – because if you are in Christ, you are on the other side of God's scales. You are in him, and therefore you will not be found wanting. That is the gospel. That is the good news! Belshazzar had defied God for too long; he had gone too far, there was no hope, and God could only judge. But God's day of grace is still open. If you feel that your life would not stand up to balancing *against* Christ, then get *into* Christ, have him as your Saviour and Lord, and God will never have to write on the wall for you.

6

DEN OF LIONS
Read Daniel 6

Prologue (1–3) – Daniel exalted
A. PLOT FASHIONED (4–13)
      1. Darius's pride (4–9)
      2. Daniel's prayer (10–11)
B. PLOT FOILED (14–24)
      1. Darius's predicament (14–18)
      2. Daniel's protection (19–24)
Epilogue (25–28) – Daniel's God exalted

Now we come to the last of the stories about Daniel in the book of Daniel, even though we are only halfway through it. You probably know how Daniel, thrown into the lions' den, was delivered by God. Again, I want to begin by stating that we are dealing here with fact and not fiction. A number of scholars and critics of the Bible have thought that this passage is a legend. They say that primarily for one reason and I mention it in case anybody uses this in an argument with you against Daniel. They say, "There is no trace whatever of King Darius in secular records. Archeologists have never come across his name." Indeed, the records say that Cyrus the Persian was the first king of Babylon after it was defeated. So the scholars and critics have almost verged on the malicious and the vicious in their criticism of Daniel 6. It prompted one Christian to write a book called "Daniel in the Critic's Den", and I think Daniel will come out of that den as well as he came out of the other one! But, funnily enough, it was exactly the same problem as the critics found with Daniel 5. They said, "There is no trace whatever of the name Belshazzar outside the Bible and therefore we don't believe he existed." I have already explained how that one has been dealt with – for now the archeologists have discovered the name Belshazzar inscribed in cuneiform writing on a tablet of stone. The critics have been seen to be wrong about chapter five. Now I have to be absolutely honest with you and state that as yet we have not discovered Darius's name in secular records. But frankly, I would have thought that what has happened with chapter five should keep us quiet about chapter six. Let us just hang on a while and let the archeologists go on digging with their spades, shall we? I have found that this kind of criticism, this kind of attack on the Bible, is neutralised by time and that if we only hold on until we know a bit more and not jump to conclusions we find ourselves bowing before the Word of God.

So at the moment we have no evidence outside the Bible for King Darius but then we didn't have for Pontius Pilate, we didn't have for Belshazzar and a host of others, all of whom have been proved to be real people. So I am prepared to wait. But I believe we are dealing here with fact, not fiction, and that one day we will find out that Darius was a real character, and we will certainly find out that Daniel was, and I believe the lions were too.

The most extraordinary feature of this chapter is something that I had not realised until I really got into this book, and that is this marvellous truth: that Daniel was over ninety years of age when this happened. We think of ninety year olds as marvellous if they are just surviving, especially the men. We are not the stronger sex after sixty-five. The fact that Daniel wasn't dead at ninety is marvellous, and the fact that he was not doddery is even more marvellous, and the fact that he was prime minister is even more wonderful – and the fact that he has not hung onto office long after he is too old to do the job.

It is marvellous that with a whole empire from which to choose, an emperor who wanted the job done efficiently chose a ninety-three year old because he was a man of integrity, a man in whom there is an excellent spirit, says the Bible, a man who can be trusted, a man who has got energy and ability; a man who is still going strong and who had seen all the kings come and go. We had such a man in our former church. He was ninety-two. A fortnight older or younger than Churchill but just about the same age at that time. When he was told that Churchill had died he said, "Well I'm not surprised. He's been a heavy smoker and drinker all his life." Joe Stevens went into the garden and tripped over a garden rake and came furious into the house and said, "Who left that rake there? I might have been disfigured for life!" That was his spirit and he was another Daniel, for he was a man who walked with the Lord and lived with the Lord and prayed to the Lord right through his life. It is tremendous when you meet a live Daniel, a man who is still going strong, still witnessing, still walking with God.

Of course, it is not always given to the saints to have a long life, but to those whom God gives this gift, what a wonderful testimony someone like this can be. So get rid of the Sunday school pictures, which show a rather smart young man lying with his head on a nice lion, warm and snug in a lions' den. Think of a man of ninety-three, a man who has been walking with the Lord since his earliest years, a man who (as a sixteen-year old, remember) showed that he chose God's way, a man who has walked with the Lord all those years. So he was chosen to head up the civil service of the new Medo-Persian Empire.

I recall a person in my congregation once who left to take a very important civil service position in the Midlands. I asked him if he would show me his application form for the post because I heard something about it on the grapevine. When he wrote to apply for this job and had to say how he would set about organising it, he quoted Daniel 6 to those future employers of his and said, "Well here's an Old Testament precedent of good organisation, and I think this is the kind of administration I would want to set up in the city of "X" if I get the job." He got the job, and I think it was great that Daniel 6 could get someone a job in the civil service in these days!

Here is the biblical ground for good organisation, and Darius, the new conqueror, wanted to organise the empire well. He divided it into 120 districts, and each of those had a satrap over them – that was their name for an official. There were three presidents over the 120, and he got it well organised. The one thing he was trying to get over was corruption. Reading between the lines of the Hebrew language at this point, it is saying that there was an awful lot of lining people's pockets. Money was talking too much. He wanted an administration that was above corruption. So he deliberately organised the empire this way and said, "Who can I choose to head up my administration?" When he searched the empire, he found a man of God to do this. Daniel's testimony here was clear, and he was chosen to head this up because of his qualities.

When you are promoted it is almost certain that other people will be envious and will not like you as much as they did when you worked alongside them, especially if you are different. It does not pay to be different in our world. If you are a man of God, you will be different. I have no doubt of the three reasons why the other officials in the civil service of Darius began to get very envious and malicious towards Daniel. Reason number one: he had been promoted and they hadn't. Consider his age. "Fancy choosing that old boy!" It may not be easy for forty year olds with big families to look after, working their way up, to see a man of ninety-three get the job. You can understand all the feelings here. The second reason would be his nationality – he was a foreigner. The third reason was that you couldn't get any bribery and corruption past Daniel, and therefore it began to go. These three things combined caused there to be real enemies of Daniel, and they began to meet together in a conspiracy to plot against this man. How could they get rid of him?

Here comes the most marvellous thing in this chapter. I don't think the most marvellous thing is the lions keeping their mouths shut. I think the most marvellous thing is this: that they studied Daniel carefully and closely and they could not find a single thing that they could tell tales about to Darius. There was no error, no fault, no mistake. What we are saying is that a commission of government agents set up to investigate the background of Daniel could find nothing anywhere back in his whole life. They could find no witness who would say, "Well he did this, or he did that" – not one. It is a remarkable situation. They studied everything he had done in the empire, every position he had held, and they had to admit that they could not find a thing that they could blow up or exaggerate and use as a handle against Daniel. So they said, "There's only one way to do it, and that is through his religion."

Let me tell you about an incident involving my father because he found this when he was promoted and when he was given a certain job as a lecturer in a university. Because he was a Christian and because he went out preaching on Sundays, there were undercurrents. Finally, a complaint was lodged with the head of the department that his Christian activity was causing his work to suffer and that his preaching was bound to affect his lecturing. So my father was brought before the head of the department. Do you know what happened? It was pointed out by someone, quite simply, that my father was always the first one in his office on Monday morning before anybody else. The whole thing was dropped, just like that.

You see, they were trying to get him on the religious side. They were trying to engineer something and say that preaching the gospel was causing the lecturing to suffer, but there was a testimony that somebody else gave: always first in the office before all the others who had spent the Sunday down at the seashore or washing their cars or doing their gardens.

These are important things we are looking at now. So people said, "Look we can't find anything to pin on Daniel except his religion. How can we trap him in this? Can we say something that will be able to suggest that his religion is affecting his work?" They began to plot, and you know that the plot is diabolical.

Satan put within men's minds a devilish plot that was certain to succeed because it was based on Darius's pride and Daniel's prayer, and those were two things they knew about and put the two together. Let us see how the plot was worked out. They went to Darius and said, "King Darius" – it is said that they rushed into it, all of them surged into the room as if they were terribly excited, and they said – "King Darius we've had a great idea. We want to suggest something to you that will really establish your reign in our land. We want to suggest that you become the high priest of all the religions of the empire, and that for one whole month all prayer is addressed to you."

Now such things seem strange to us. I once had lunch with the Dalai Lama and it seemed so strange to me that people regarded this man as a god-king. I could no more have thought of praying to him than flying. To me he was just a man for whom Christ died. But when you read books about Tibetan life you realise that their belief is that this man is an incarnation of a god, and that he is the great high priest of their religion, and that prayer should be addressed through him! (By the way, I gave him a copy of the Bible and prayed that the Holy Spirit will open his mind to its wonderful truth.) But, you see, here was a king who was a god, an incarnation, and therefore revered and even worshipped. It is not a strange idea in the East, though it is odd to us. We wouldn't think of saying, "For one month all prayers must be addressed to the Prime Minister." You may laugh at that because the idea seems so ridiculous. But this suggestion was very normal to the king: you become the high priest of all religions and you can unite the empire, and people will come and pray through you and to you.

Darius thought: that's a great idea, I'll not only be king, I'll be a god-king, and it appealed tremendously to his vanity.

It got him. They only told one little lie to get him. Do you know what the lie was? "All of us have agreed." They should have said "all but one". That was all they needed to say to get the thing through. Darius only needed to say: you want to treat me as god-king, fine, let's do it; good idea, we'll get all these religions united and I'll be the high priest of them all. You can see it happening. So he signed it in a hurry.

Lesson number one for all of us is this: Satan likes you to do things in a hurry. He hates you to sleep on a problem, hates you to think it over, think out the implications and consequences of what you are doing, and believe me, the decisions most of us have made that we have regretted have been decisions we have made in a hurry. People rushed us into it and it appealed to us, it fitted in with our ideas and we said, "Right let's do it." The king pulled out his pen immediately and said, "Let's sign it – great." It was signed and done. Little did he know what the result would be.

Now the other half of the plot depended on Daniel's prayer. Here we are going to touch one of the secrets of this ninety-three year old man. What was his secret? It was not only that he ate good food for his body. He was a vegetarian, as you know – not that that is a principle, but you know why he did it in that land. He lived on vegetables and water rather than meat and wine for his life. But what was his secret? I'll tell you. He got three good *spiritual* meals per day. That was his secret: morning, noon, and night, three times a day, Daniel fed his soul. Here we are going to learn some things about Daniel's prayer life. First of all, when did he pray? Three times a day as his custom was. He did not start praying when the trouble came, his prayer was backbone rather than wishbone – do you understand that statement? He didn't wait till the storm came to get his anchor down. He had got it down already. He prayed before he was thrown into the lions' den, and therefore when he was thrown into the lions' den he just went on praying. I love this statement, that Daniel simply went on as normal.

Now there are two rules in the Bible about praying: number one, shut your door; number two, open your windows. I want to say a little more about these two rules now. When you pray, get into a private place, secretly, where nobody can see you. I have sometimes advised young men going into the forces against the advice given to them by their church. They were so often told by a senior Christian: "When you get into the barracks, when you get into the forces, the first night get on your knees, in front of them all, get your flag up, get your standard set," but Jesus taught that is not the way to show people you are a Christian. Don't pray in public. Don't parade your prayer. It is the most dangerous thing to do, because if you do it you will find you are thinking more of the people watching you than you are of God. So Daniel went upstairs to his bedroom, which was on the roof, and he shut the door – that is the first rule in prayer. Private prayer should not be seen or known by anyone else. "Shut the door," said Jesus, shut yourself in with God, but then open your windows towards Jerusalem.

Daniel was doing something the scriptures had told him to do, because King Solomon, when the temple was built, had prayed something like this: "And Lord, when your people are taken away to a land far away because of their sin, if they pray toward this place then hear from heaven and save them." Do you pray opening your windows to Jerusalem – not the one on earth but the one up in heaven? I think it is a more helpful gesture to pray with your knees bent but your head up, and that was how Daniel prayed: face set towards the place where he knew God was.

A little child once said to me after a service I had taken, "I know where God is." When asked where, the child said, "He's up at the back of the gallery in the church."

"Why do you think he's there?"

"Because that's where the preacher's face is looking."

But, in fact, when Jesus prayed he lifted up his eyes to heaven. He looked up. Knees down, head up – that was how Daniel prayed. Door shut, windows open. In other words, turn your back on the world. Shut the world out but open up to God—that is how to pray.

You notice that Daniel, knowing that he was about to be thrown into the lions' den, began his prayer with "Thank you". Have you noticed that in the Bible? He prayed with thanksgiving. What was he thanking God for? For the lions? For the decree? For his enemies? I believe he was. Have you discovered the secret of praising God when you are in difficulty? Have you discovered the secret of really wanting to say, "Please, please, please..." and learning to say, "Thank you, thank you, thank you." That is a tremendous secret of prayer. If you study this little section on Daniel's teaching on prayer, you will discover the secret of a man of ninety-three going straight to the lions. Daniel was a Daniel in his bedroom before he was a Daniel in the den—that is the lesson of Daniel 6.

So you can imagine the scene: Daniel is in his bedroom, the door is shut, the windows are open, and on the next-door roof there is a crowd of people peering through the lattice, waiting for him to pray. The one thing they are quite sure of (notice this): Daniel will obey God rather than men. They can only trap him because of his integrity. I find that marvellous. They were sure he would pray, and pray he did. There are times when Christians have to break the law. There are times when men's decrees must be set aside. There are times when we must obey God rather than men, and this is one of them. If a law were to be passed forbidding Christians to meet together in this land, as such laws have been passed elsewhere, then we would have to meet together even if it meant the lions. Daniel's prayer, I am afraid, led him into the plot.

Now let us look at the second half: the plot foiled. An impossible situation, it looks as if there is no way out of Darius's predicament. There is something terribly sad about a ruler enmeshed by his own wrong decisions but also enmeshed in his own legal system. Nebuchadnezzar would never have been caught like this. He would have simply abolished the law. In God's sight, Nebuchadnezzar was a better sovereign than Darius because Nebuchadnezzar made the laws and he was not tied. You may think that is immoral, but in fact in God's sight, a ruler who is at the mercy of his people is not a very pleasant sight. But Nebuchadnezzar was a golden sovereign as we saw in chapter two, and he really did reign. He would not have allowed his own laws to make him do something immoral. He would have said, "It's wrong – I abolish the law."

But not so Darius. Darius is one step down in God's scale of sovereignty, and Darius has made a law and they said that the law of the Medes and the Persians cannot be altered. You can't sack the prosecutor and you can't dismiss the commission and you can't get out of this. You made the law and you have tied yourself. Darius was not a big enough man to say, "Then the law I made was wrong. I have made a wrong decision and I get out of that situation and do it with sovereign might."

All night long there would have been secret meetings with his legal advisors. He tried so hard to find a loophole, another law to get him out of it, and all the time he could have said, "I am responsible only to God, and I did the wrong thing in signing that decree and it's better for me to break my own law than to throw Daniel to the lions." Sometimes we have to break our foolish oaths and promises that have led us into wrongdoing. There are plenty of cases in the Bible like this.

Do you remember the man who foolishly promised that if God gave him victory the first living thing he saw on his farm when he got home would be sacrificed to God? Do you remember that silly man? He made an oath to God and do you know when he came back to his farm after the battle, the first living thing he saw was his own daughter!

The Bible talks about the folly of making these immoral oaths. When Darius saw the 120 satraps and the two presidents he couldn't find a legal way around the matter. He had Daniel thrown into the lions' den. The only little hope there was, the only little spark of faith in Darius's heart, was this: he said to Daniel, "Maybe your God will help, maybe your God can deliver you." Had he heard about Shadrach, Meshach, and Abednego? I don't know. But he was trapped. Daniel, you pray to your God and he might do something.

So we find Daniel in the lions' den. The king couldn't get to sleep – no wonder, for he was trapped. I believe that this is what was happening in the lions' den: imagine a pit with two compartments and a gate in between them, used to entice the lions from one to the other with food, and to clean it out. There was a hole at the top and they used to let down the victims with rope slings under their arms. There was a door in the side. When they threw Daniel in that den they sealed that door in the side with a stone and the king's seal. That reminds me of something. As Jesus would come out of a tomb, Daniel would come out of this den. While the poor king had been tossing and turning on his bed, I guess Daniel was just having a lovely little sleep in the corner of the den. I think all the lions were in the other corner because, believe me, animals are sometimes more aware of supernatural things than we human beings are. I have known situations where an animal has been aware of supernatural beings where men have not been. Balaam's ass is a case in point. There is old Balaam whipping his ass to go on down the road, and the ass won't move. Why not? Because there is an angel standing down the road, and animals are extraordinarily sensitive. Sometimes before an earthquake hits a city the dogs and the cats will start making strange noises and run. Animals are sensitive.

In that den, Daniel was not alone. "My God sent his angel," he said. The angel stood between Daniel and the lions, and the lions stayed in their corner. Spurgeon's explanation – that the lions didn't eat Daniel because most of him was backbone and the rest of him was grit – is probably a bit of bad exegesis. The real reason was that those lions were sensitive to supernatural power. The angel stood between Daniel and the lions.

Some years ago I read a book about a missionary. That man of God was told to go and visit a certain village and preach. To get there he had to wade across a river which was infested with crocodiles. The people who were with him saw him wade into the river and saw the crocodiles surging through the water, making straight for him. This man just quietly said to the crocodiles, "In the name of Jesus, go." The watchers saw the crocodiles turn around and go away from that man. You see, God is in control. Those rulers of this world who are like Darius are nothing.

When God is in control and intervenes supernaturally, neither animal nor man can touch a man of God. In fact Jesus said you could pick up snakes. That doesn't teach us to go around picking up every snake we see, but it does say that he can protect. David Livingstone was attacked by lions in the jungle, but God was with him. Only years later, when his body was brought to the coast of Africa and shipped back to England to be buried in Westminster Abbey, there were many sceptics who doubted if it was Livingstone until they saw the marks of the lion claws on his body. Then they knew it was him. There in Westminster Abbey lies a man of God who was delivered from the lions in Africa.

That is not to say that everybody is delivered from the lions. For every Livingstone, for every Daniel, there have been men and women who have been thrown to the lions in the name of Christ and have been torn limb from limb as they sang hymns to our Lord. I stood in the ruins of the Colosseum in the centre of Rome, and I thought of the blood of Christians in that arena when they set the lions on them. I looked at the dens of the lions there. Yes, God has different ways of dealing with people, but God can send his angel to shut the lions' mouths.

The lions lost their appetite on this night. Think of the dramatic scene. The king comes before it is light. He hasn't slept a wink and it says he ran to the den. See the man, he is pale, sleepless, bags under his eyes, he shouts in the darkness, "Daniel, Daniel" – he doesn't expect an answer: "Daniel, did your God do anything for you?" Then there is a voice. Daniel quietly says, "Darius, I did nothing wrong against you. I have done nothing wrong against God so I'm still here." What a moment! They let down the ropes and pulled him up. Darius, in his fury, really saw now where he stood and how he had been trapped by evil, malicious men. He said, "Throw them in. They believe in their gods, let's see what their gods can do now. Throw them in." It sounds vicious, it sounds an act of revenge, yet I think if you lived in the Middle East you would understand this reaction. They had been perfectly happy to throw a ninety-three year old man of God to the lions and see him torn limb from limb – terrible. As they let the men down into the den, the lions jumped up at them and were tearing their limbs to pieces before their feet touched the floor. It proves that the lions were hungry.

So they came to the end to which all enemies of the people of God will come. I tremble for anyone who sets themselves against a man of God because he will come to a terrible end and everything he wishes on the man of God will come back on himself. It backfires in a horrible way. The result is that Daniel's God is exalted. That is the finest thing in the story. This account is not so that you may praise Daniel. It finishes up saying: Isn't God wonderful? He is a God who delivers his people. His kingdom is everlasting. His power is unlimited. King Darius sends a decree out to the whole empire: Daniel's God is to be feared and worshipped. Here is Darius, who thought he was god and wanted people to pray to him, now saying: "You pray to this God."

God has humbled this man through the testimony of a ninety-three year old saint. Think of who God could speak to through you. There are lions that you are going to face. There are lions in the shape of men. When Paul was on trial in Rome, everybody deserted him. He had no witness for the defence – not one. I don't know where the Christians went to or whether they were afraid of being caught up in it. But when Paul went on trial in Rome he stood in the dock and the judges said, "Any witnesses for the defendant?" There were none. Yet the verdict was not guilty and he was released and he went on further travels and wrote further letters.

When he wrote to Timothy, he was writing a letter after his imprisonment in Rome and after his release, and talking of the trial he said, "When I was on trial no one stood by me but God delivered me from the lion's mouth." Isn't that a tremendous statement? For in fact they did use lions in Rome as punishment. They did throw people to the lions but God delivered him from the lion's mouth. I think he is referring to the Roman emperor. When you are all alone, dare to be a Daniel and dare to stand alone. Paul stood alone in the courtroom in Rome.

There is one other lion I want to mention because you are going to meet him this week. Peter wrote a letter saying the devil is like a prowling lion wandering around seeking someone to devour. What would you do if you walked out of church one day and saw a lion just outside? What would you do? You have heard about the two lions walking along Oxford Street and one said to the other, "I thought this place was supposed to be crowded!" If there were lions around us, I'll tell you what we would do – we would watch. There was a lioness set free by accident. The police were going round the area saying "Stay indoors." When I travelled up the railway from Mombasa to Nairobi, I was told how there were so many lions that this was the biggest difficulty in building that railway. Half the men had to stay on watch because of the prowling lions, to get that railway built. You know what Peter says in his letter – the devil is like a prowling lion seeking someone to devour. You are going to be thrown to the lion this week. You live in the devil's world and he is like a prowling lion and it is unsafe for you to be wandering around in this world with that prowling lion. The way that Daniel met those lions is the way that you will meet this one. It is in that bedroom with the shut door and the open window. It is in that facing towards Jerusalem. No matter what your position, what your promotion, thank God that when Daniel went up and up the social ladder, and up in promotion, his religion never suffered. He went on building himself up for the day that was going to come – when the moment came and he would be thrown into that den. What a lesson this is for us! The devil is like a prowling lion. You need the hosts of God between you and that evil intelligence, but believe me, the Word of God says that angels can shut that lion's mouth and he can't touch the Daniels. Dare to be a Daniel; dare to stand alone.

7

BEASTLY DREAM
Read Daniel 7

A. THE APPARITION (1–14)
    1. Monsters rising (2–8)
    2. Majesty descending (9–14)
B. THE APPLICATION (15–28)
    1. Kings of earth (15–25)
    2. Kingdom of heaven (26–28)
        a. Ancient of Days
        b. Son of Man
        c. Saints of the Most High

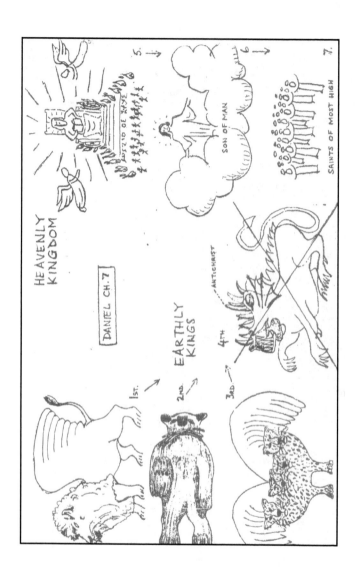

With the second half of Daniel we get into a very different section of this book. For one thing, the narrative changes from the third person to the first, from talking about Daniel as "he" to Daniel talking about himself as "I" — much more personal. We are reading Daniel's own diary. Daniel kept a diary by his bed and filled it up, writing down everything that happened.

We are also changing from a report of things that are past to a report of things that are future, and only the Word of God can do this. Other *people* may speculate and guess and study the stars, but only God can tell us exactly what is going to happen in the future. So chapters one to six were all written up after the events they described whereas chapters seven to twelve are written up before the events they describe – that makes it a fascinating subject.

Then we have changed from straightforward stories about things that happened, Daniel in the lions' den, Shadrach, Meshach, and Abednego in the fiery furnace, and we have switched to vision and dream. From now on the book is very much in picture language. Now Daniel had a dream and he was quite unable to interpret it for himself, having interpreted dreams for Nebuchadnezzar and others. He could not for himself discover the meaning of the dream he had, but very few dreams that we have are unrelated to real life. Usually some thoughts or experiences, or something we have seen during the day, comes into our dream at night. God is able to weave these things into his pattern and his message. The significant thing is that Daniel had this dream in the first year of Belshazzar the king. Now why would that cause him to dream like this? Very simply, Daniel saw what maybe others had not seen, that with the arrival of this playboy prince called Belshazzar, the empire that had already stood firm for seventy years was going to crumble.

He realised that a ruler like this, of this weakness, of this self-indulgence, would spell the death of the empire of Babylon. Remember, Daniel had been in this empire since his early teens right through to old age. He had known little else, and suddenly he sees that the world he has known is crumbling; it is finished. A sense of deep insecurity may have come into his heart, the kind of insecurity I am meeting in many hearts today, particularly among older people who realise that the world they knew, even the churches they knew, are disappearing fast. There is a deep sense of the passing nature of this scene we call history.

Daniel went to bed and he dreamt, and in the dream God assured him about the future and revealed to him something which he not only saw in the dream itself, but when he woke up he saw it again in a vision. The word "vision" in the Bible always means something you see when you are awake, and "dream" always means something when you are asleep. Both can be of the Holy Spirit, and when the Holy Spirit is poured out on men and women, then old men dream dreams and young men see visions, and these two forms of picture language come alive, and God uses them to speak. Daniel had a dream that night and God drew back the curtain that hides the future from our natural intelligence. Maybe that is why it came in a dream, because if it had first come when his critical faculties were awake he might have argued. He might have refused to accept it. But somehow in a dream you accept the oddest things, don't you? You accept them as normal. Indeed, you find yourself, even in a dream, talking to people in the dream and asking questions. That is what Daniel did here. He asked one of the angels that he saw in the dream what it all meant, and the angel told him. But when he woke up he saw it all again, vividly. So he took his bedside diary and wrote it down, and here we have it now – part of the Word of God for us. We are going to look, then, at this dream and what it is all about.

Let me begin by looking at the outline of this chapter. The dream itself divides very neatly into seven actual features, and they divide easily into a group of four and another of three.

In the first group we have four extraordinary animals first. Then the dream switches totally and he sees three human figures. He sees a very old man called "The Ancient of days", a younger man called "Son of Man", and a lot of human beings called "saints of the Most High".

So the first part of the dream is animals and the second part of the dream looks like human beings, but we will have to look more closely at that later. The contrast between the first and second part of the dream is quite great. For example, in the first part of the dream the animals come out of the sea from below – they are rising up. In the second part of the dream, the figures he sees are all caught up with clouds – the sky rather than the sea is the backcloth to the second half, and something is coming down. In the one case, there are monsters rising, but in the other case, as I have indicated, there is majesty descending. Furthermore, the four animals are ferocious brutes which attack others, and each of them in turn seems to do damage and then fade, until the fourth one comes, and that is the worst of all.

So the first part of the dream has a horrible, threatening kind of atmosphere. The second half is comforting and seems to be encouraging. Even though it is a bit of a nightmare, Daniel finishes up pale of countenance, it is true, but somewhat reassured that the dream did have a happy ending, or at least a holy ending, as we are going to see. Now that is the dream – fairly simple, seven things, four and then three.

What is the meaning of the dream? We must now turn to the application.

Daniel, unable to understand his dream, has to ask for an interpretation. We will start as he started, with the four horrible animals and ask what they are. We have an advantage over Daniel because we have more than a diary in which to record dreams. We have a Bible which includes the book of Revelation, or the book of the unveiling of the future, the book of the apocalypse – which means to draw back the curtain. In that book, particularly in chapters thirteen and fourteen, we discover a commentary on Daniel and on these very animals, and particularly on the fourth. So we have help from the rest of the Bible. The more I study this book, the more I discover that the Bible interprets itself.

The more you know this book the less you will need other books to tell you what it is about. You find that the more you read, this bit of the Old Testament enlightens this bit of the New and vice versa. The book of Revelation is a fuller commentary on the book of Daniel. The two are related very closely. Let us look at these animals. The angel says they represent empires and rulers. It is not an unusual thing for an empire to choose a grotesque, hybrid animal to represent itself. Think of the unicorn for example. Maybe you don't often think of that, but a unicorn doesn't exist yet it is there as a grotesque animal which nevertheless represents the British empire, our crown – the lion and the unicorn together. On the gates of Ishtar outside Babylon, one of the animals is depicted which was made up of a snake's head, a lion's body, and eagle's claws and feet. These four strange, hybrid creatures made up of bits of other animals represent, quite simply, empires and rulers on the earth. The sea, the turbulent ocean with winds blowing from north, south, east, west – the Bible says four winds from every direction are blowing. It is almost a hurricane: wind coming in from all directions and stirring up the sea. This represents the turbulent history of men, the seething mass of humanity constantly changing, and the world of history and the map of our world changes almost as rapidly as the weather does. If you buy an atlas, it will be out of date in five years. The boundaries will have been redrawn. It is rather like the forecasters' weather charts you see on television each night. So out of this seething mass, with the winds blowing and stirring things up, arise four animals. Now what do the winds stand for? The Bible doesn't say, but I'm going to make a guess at it. The word "wind" in the Bible is the same as the word "spirit" and the word "breath". Here we have four winds, or four spirits if you like, blowing; here we have the influence on human affairs of evil spirits blowing on our history, stirring up all kinds of things, and raising all kinds of brutal creatures. So out of this seething mass of human history – stirred up into turbulence by the evil spirits that do surround us and have a very real part in our affairs – there come four beasts or animals. Now who are they? What empires are represented?

At this point I have to be honest and tell you that there has been a traditional interpretation, which has held sway for many a long day, which is normally accepted as the right one but which I am afraid I am convinced is wrong, but I had better deal with it first because you may have been brought up on this one.

The traditional interpretation is that chapter two and chapter seven are dealing with the same empires. Do you remember that big giant, the big beast of Nebuchadnezzar's dream – the head and shoulders, the chest and arms, the loins, and then the legs, representing the four empires of Babylon, Persia, Greece, and Rome? Now undoubtedly that is what is represented in chapter two. People have said, "Couldn't this be the same? Couldn't these four animals be Babylon (and Babylon was very fond of the symbolism of a lion) and

Persia, then Greece, and could that very fierce one represent Roman might?" Well, it could. But there are at least four major reasons why it couldn't. I give you these reasons now so that you can rethink the position and then we will get back to a positive identification. The first reason is that the history of those four empires does not fit the details of these animals. There are many major discrepancies. For example, Rome never was ruled over by ten rulers – the Roman Empire never had ten horns. Greece never started with four heads. It started with one head, Alexander the Great, whereas this beast has four heads from the beginning. There are many other discrepancies. Perhaps the outstanding discrepancy is that these empires did not arise in a period of international turbulence.

The second main reason is this: Persia and Greece are mentioned by name in chapter eight, and Persia is said to be like a ram and Greece is said to be like a goat. Now God is getting thoroughly mixed up if he is calling them something else here. The third reason is even more cogent: that Daniel is told in the dream that all four of these beasts shall arise in the future, whereas when Daniel had this dream, Babylon is already on the way out and is past, so it can't be that.

The final deciding argument for me is verse 12 which says that the first three beasts, though they lose their world dominion, will survive the extinction of the fourth – clearly stated in the Bible. So the lion, the bear and the panther represent empires that will still be there when the fourth empire has been utterly destroyed and has vanished. Now clearly you just cannot fit Babylon, Persia, Greece, and Rome into these four.

Turning to positive identification, I am now going to start with the fourth beast because it is the easiest one to identify. It is the clearest – there are most clues. It is the most important of the four. In fact, twenty-one verses are given to us about this beast and only three verses about these three. So clearly the focus of the whole dream is on that beast. That is the most important feature of the whole dream. Here the book of Revelation comes to my aid: it speaks of the last world empire of human history as a beast with ten kings. The very last empire of all that human history will ever see is a kingdom with ten beasts. Now are we on to something? Furthermore, Revelation says this extraordinary thing: that this beast will have learned certain things from previous empires and will therefore be made up of a lion's mouth, a leopard's body, and a bear's feet. It is intriguing that this final world empire will have included in itself features of these three. Furthermore, Revelation tells us that out of those ten horns one will become the strongest and will become the final dictator of a world state.

The book of Revelation gives a name: Antichrist. The word "anti" by the way doesn't mean *against*; it means *instead of*. So Antichrist is called "Instead of Christ" – the last world dictator. I tell you with certainty, one day there will be a dictator controlling the whole world. The Bible says that is the final stage of world history – a dictator who has got there by ruthless, vicious, cruel methods, destroying all opposition, hence the iron teeth and the brass claws of this last beast. Well now, if this is so, we have identified the fourth beast. We shall know when this beast appears in human history. Mark my words, at the end of history there will be an empire with ten rulers.

Daniel says that of those ten, three will be rooted out of their countries, of their states if you like, within the world empire, and one little horn starting small will grow, take over those three first, and then dominate the other seven and take over as world dictator. When you see that happen you will know we are in the very last part of human history. Certain things are said about this little horn, this evil man who controls everything. He has got a big mouth and hypnotic eyes so he will be just right for radio and television. He will most certainly use both to establish worldwide dominion. We are told that he will seek to do what they tried to do in the French Revolution: to change godly laws and times and seasons and days. I will tell you one of the things he will do: he will abolish the seven-day week. Sunday will go, disappearing altogether. In the French Revolution they tried a ten-day week to get rid of Sunday. That is exactly what this man will do, and God's laws of marriage (as monogamy between a man and a woman for life) he will change.

All the laws of God that tell us how to run human affairs he will change because he is Antichrist and wants to make the laws for us instead of Christ. Sadly, it says too here that he will make war on the saints. The people of God are going to suffer terribly under this final beast. But, praise God, God has said: I have limited those days; I've shortened them – three and a half years and they are finished; that's as much as I will allow him. That period of three and a half years is mentioned in the book of Revelation frequently – sometimes as three and a half years, sometimes as forty-two months, and sometimes as an equivalent number of days.

You get this clear period in which the people of God suffer terribly. The book of Revelation reveals, for example, that people will have to have a number on their foreheads to get into a shop to buy food. No doubt it will go onto our numbered account, but we are told that we will have to have a number just to buy food, and that the saints of God will not be given that number and will not accept it. Can you imagine what that is going to mean for family life? This is this final beast, and the book of Revelation unfolds in far greater detail just what Daniel is talking about. We speak about this as the period of the "big trouble" or in Bible language "Great tribulation".

Now I think there can be no doubt that we have identified the strange creature I call the "griffin", that hybrid beast in Daniel's dream/vision. This is not the Roman empire, which has long since gone. This is the last empire of world history, the very climax of Satan's power in this world, when Satan puts a human dictator over the whole affair. In a sense, one prays that neither oneself nor one's children will be alive when that happens. There are indications that we may very well be – God prepare us for it. Having identified the fourth of course, I haven't done it precisely. I haven't been able to tell you which ruler, in which country, this Antichrist will appear. He has not yet appeared, but people are prone to pick out this and that world leader and see in them the Antichrist. John the apostle said there are many antichrists gone out in the world – but not the big one yet. There are many antichrists all around, people who would love to be Christ, people who would love to be the "saviour" of their people. There are those who love to be worshipped, people who love to make the laws and change them. There are many antichrists, but the one who is coming hasn't come yet. When he does I won't need to tell you who he is. From what I have told you, you will know already, and you will know that we are in the last minutes.

What about the other three then? These are three world powers which will rise to power before this one does, which will lose their power but still be there identifiably as nations when this one comes, and will survive right through, and still be there after this one has been crossed out. Are there any clues about these? The one biblical principle we must apply is this: all the nations and empires mentioned in the Bible are those that have dealings with God's Holy Land in some way. That is why, for example, China is never mentioned in the Bible. It has never had dealings with the Holy Land. That is why America is never mentioned directly in the

Bible. Therefore we must look for nations that have had direct dealings with Jerusalem, with Israel, with the Holy Land. It is true that Babylon, Persia, Greece and Rome all did, and therefore that is why they are mentioned in Daniel chapter 2, but are there any empires or nations of today that fit any of these symbols?

What I am going to offer you now is my own personal opinion. It could be dismissed as speculation too, but I feel I ought to offer it to you. What empire could be symbolised by a lion that has had dealings with Jerusalem? The answer is: the British Empire. From 1917, when General Allenby walked into Jerusalem, until 1948 when we walked out, we were responsible for the holy city of God. Whether we liked it or not, we were drawn into the Middle East. I know we made contradictory promises to Arab and Jew, and that is why we don't have the confidence of either now. But nevertheless, we were responsible; we were drawn in. We therefore, I believe, became part of God's history at that point. Now if that is so we could be looking at ourselves in this chapter.

Where would the eagle's wings fit in? As the lion is king of the beasts, the eagle is king of the birds, and the eagle's wings could in this instance refer to America, since time and again the might and the flight of America to us has saved us from disaster. We must acknowledge that the English-speaking Western world has been involved together, but the interesting part of this vision is this: the wings and the lion are separated from one another and begin to act independently. The lion is without the wings. The British lion, which was given such a vast empire throughout the world, has now been cut down to the size of a human nation. We are no longer a world power and we have got to face it. We are just the height of a man right now, and we are being treated that way. That is why the Africans talk about the toothless lion. We are no longer a power to be feared or reckoned with. Is this the meaning of the first beast? If so, then let us move on to the second and ask what empire there is that is symbolised by a bear, that is getting interested in the Middle East and beginning to affect God's people there. The answer seems to me as clear as daylight – Russia. The bear is an ungainly animal. It is clumsy but it makes up in ferocity what it lacks in cunning. It attacks people by sheer weight and strength.

One of the most interesting phrases in the Hebrew is that it is a bear raised up on one side, stretching out one paw in one direction as if it is frightened to stretch out in the other direction, which to me would be very simply explained by the Russian bear reaching into Europe with its great claws. We have seen those ribs in the bear's mouth, but on the other side not daring to stretch a paw against China. Is this correct?

The proof of the identification would be this: if what I have said about the lion and the bear is correct, then I can with confidence say this will come next, for I see no empire on earth to correspond at the moment to the panther with four rulers. But if within the next few years we see the rise of a world power led by four rulers together, "holding the world to ransom" it says, then I think you can accept that these two are probably the correct identification. I would therefore say: watch the Arab world. The Hebrew here says they will have the power to hold the rest of the world to ransom, this beast. The Arabs are already beginning to show us that this could be. I say: watch the Middle East.

There is something else that I can tell you about this third beast which I do not yet see anywhere in the world. Do you remember the four winds at the beginning that stirred up the sea? It says the four winds – that means the north, south, east, and west winds. If the lion is the British Empire then it came from the west to the Middle East. If Russia is the bear it came from the north. Therefore the others must come from the south or the east of the Holy Land. Therefore I look for that coming from south or east and taking over the situation and holding the rest of the world at bay. I admit this is human opinion. I think it has got a good deal more to say for it then trying to fit Babylon, Persia, Greece, and Rome into a pattern that does not fit.

What I can say quite dogmatically is this: these are the last four world powers that will affect the Middle East directly. When these things happen we know where we are in history. We have got the Word of God and there is everything we need to be aware of to know where we are. So I am waiting to see, and if things turn out as the Bible says in that picture, if that comes clearly on to the scene, then I know that we are getting very near to God's climax of history. We could be right in the middle of it ourselves, for the sands of time could be running out.

I turn now to the more positive side and the more wonderful side. Let us look at the other things that Daniel saw in his dream. The scene changes from earth to heaven – like the book of Revelation, the book of Daniel switches from earth to heaven. You look at earth and its troubles, and then you go up into the clouds and you see what God is thinking about it. You see, heaven and earth are connected. God is there, watching earth, controlling earth, and judging earth, and it is he who decides what happens tomorrow. It is he who allows these things to come. It is he who will bring them all to an end. Now let us look at the three things. First of all, the Ancient of Days – the only time in the Bible that God is ever pictured in a form of a human being, the only verse. God is an old man sitting on a great wheeled throne, and yet the "oldness" in that picture is not meant to convey that he is decrepit or senile. Rather, it is intended to say this: he was always there. While all these beasts came and went, while human empires rose and fell, God was always there.

The Ancient of Days – what a lovely title that is. In a

hymn we praise God, immortal, invisible, God only wise. God is the oldest ruler of earth – that is what it is saying. He has always ruled earth. You get the tremendous sense that all these beasts rising out of the sea are just playing around down here, and all the time God has been up there watching it all, controlling it all, allowing it all, knowing exactly what he would do.

The picture of God here is marvellous. There is a pile of books and God is opening them and reading them. What are they? They are the record of human deeds on earth. Whether you keep a diary of your life or not, God keeps a diary of your life. Did you realise that? In heaven there is a diary written up for every day of your life. It is interesting what you put in your own diary. Do you write your own faults and sins in your diary? It is quite a healthy practice. If you do that, you are just writing a carbon copy of God's diary about you, and God is reading books – what have they been doing on my earth? God does that before he decides what to do about people. From the throne there are thousands of angels ministering, waiting for God to give them orders, waiting for God to say: "Go down to earth and do this." Before him are gathered multitudes of people crowded around the feet of the throne. From the throne come rivers of flame, bringing down God's judgment. For fire does two things: it burns up that which is dross and rubbish, but it refines that which is precious, like gold. From the throne there comes the fire of God's judgment. It is a terrific picture. What is happening? I'll tell you what is happening. God is deciding how to dispose of human history. God is reading the books and deciding what he will do about this empire. For now the scene is the fourth beast and God is reading his books. He just has to say the word and it will be done by his messengers.

The second figure that Daniel sees is a younger person, like a Son of Man. Notice that phrase. It isn't in every translation, but it is there in the Hebrew. Someone like a Son of Man is standing on the clouds, and the clouds carry this Son of Man to the throne, and the Ancient of Days gives him a crown, and the Son of Man is carried by the clouds to earth. It is a tremendous scene. Who is this Son of Man? Jesus. Do you know that this was Jesus' favourite title for himself? Did you ever wonder why Jesus kept talking about himself as Son of Man? He was the Son of God, but he didn't go around saying the Son of God did this, that and the other. He kept saying the Son of Man came to seek what was lost; the Son of Man does this; the Son of Man does that. Where did he get that title? The answer is in the book of Daniel. My proof is not just the number of times he used it. In St Luke's Gospel alone he uses it twenty-seven times about himself, but when he stood on trial before Annas and Caiaphas (the religious part of his trial not the political), they tried to incriminate him from his own words, which was an illegal thing to do. But they said, "We adjure you by the living God, are you the Christ? Are you the Son of the living God?" Do you know what he said? "I am" – which is the name of God, and he added this: and you will see the Son of Man coming from the clouds of heaven, and he quoted this very verse. No question who the Son of Man is – it is Jesus. Therefore we are looking now at Jesus. We are looking at God here, the Ancient of Days. We are now looking at Jesus, and God has delivered to Jesus the kingdoms of the world.

Now let us move on to the third step. Just as God the Father is giving to Jesus the kingdoms of the world, Jesus is coming with clouds of glory. Have you ever seen anything more majestic than clouds? Have you ever flown above the clouds in a plane when the cumulus clouds have been built up and the sun is glistening, and you feel you are in heaven? You look out of the window and see the glory and the majesty of the billowing clouds, the colours, and the light. Do you know what God's favourite colour is? It is white. The clothes he is wearing here are white. His hair is white as snow. God made all the colours and when they come together they make white light because that is his favourite colour. It is the colour of heaven. The clouds are white with the sun shining on them, and there is the Son of Man coming.

Here is the amazing thing. The Son of Man is not going to keep that kingdom to himself. He is going to share it with other people. He is going to pass it on to the saints of the Most High, and that is the third group. Daniel sees an old man here, and it is a picture of God. He sees a young man here, and it is a picture of Jesus. He sees lots of people here, and it is a picture of the saints of the Most High. The literal truth is that the saints of the Most High, those who believe in Jesus Christ, are one day going to be the world government and reign with him after they have risen with him – that is staggering. Did you realise? Just say to yourself you are going to be a cabinet minister. I am quite serious about that: when the kingdoms of this world become the kingdom of our Christ, he is going to share that reign with his people, and we shall reign with him forever and ever.

You have heard that sung by choirs, haven't you? He shall reign forever and ever – but we shall reign with him forever and ever. It says that. Hitler boasted, like Antichrist, of a kingdom that will last a thousand years and it was gone in less than twenty. I think of Daniel 7, and how the saints will have the kingdom forever and ever. A thousand years? That is nothing to the kingdom we are going to have. Let that get right into your soul. The Ancient of Days says to the Son of Man: the kingdom is yours. The Son of Man says to the saints: the kingdom is yours. In Christ all things are ours. No speculation about this part of Daniel 7. Whether you agree with my other interpretation or not, this is the important one. This is the one that I want you to look at.

I am sure I am right about the fourth beast, and this one I am just absolutely certain about: that we shall reign with him. So we have interpreted the dream.

How practical is all this? Somebody might say: you know you have been way up in the clouds literally for me; I am muddled, perplexed and confused. How does this help me to live? I want comfort, and I want practical help for life. Now let me tell you this: I have been giving you the best help I can and the best help you need. I will tell you why – for two reasons, both beginning with "H".

First of all, I want you to have the Christian virtue of *hope*. We often neglect this. Faith, hope and love – these three are the ones that are going to abide, the virtues you can take to heaven with you. We talk a lot about faith, we talk an awful lot about love, but we are usually silent about hope, and that is one of the great three virtues of the Christian life. What I have been trying to do is strengthen your hope. I was talking to a number of couples, giving them as my text something I hear from so many people on all sides: "I don't know what things are coming to." I have never yet heard a Christian say that. Isn't that interesting? The Christian just alters it slightly and says: "I do know what things are coming to." We are the only ones in the world who do. Now that makes you able to comfort and encourage and help other people when they say, "I don't know what things are coming to." Say quietly and lovingly, "I do. Would you be interested to hear?" Tell them that one day the dictatorships of the world are going to go, and human civilisation will go, and in its place the kingdom of God will come, and Jesus is coming back to reign, and we may reign with him if we believe in him – *that* is hope. In the New Testament, hope isn't doubtful, as it is when someone says: "I hope it will happen." The word "hope" in the New Testament means "I *know* it will happen." Let us allow our hope to grow as we study these last chapters of Daniel, so that in a world that does not know where it is going and does not know what things are coming to, we can say: "We know."

The second thing is this: I hope also that this study has stimulated your *holiness*. Why? Because if you are going to reign, you had better start getting ready. Your position is that of a princess or a prince who knows that one day the responsibility of government will be yours, and the responsibility that Christ will give you in his kingdom is directly related to your faithfulness now as a Christian. If you have been faithful in much he will be able to give you much responsibility. Your position in his government depends on how you behave this week, and how you respond to his grace.

"Everyone," says the Bible, "that has this hope in him purifies himself, gets ready." I must behave as royalty. I must have the dignity of a royal child now. That is practical enough, isn't it? He is making us a kingdom of priests unto God. Then we are to live worthily and get ready for such high responsibility, and to think of the future like this and ponder frequently on our Lord's return in glory – this is to have one of the greatest stimulants to holiness that you can possibly have. Speculation? This is concern with the kitchen sink and the office desk and how you behave tomorrow morning. Isn't that thrilling? So the Word of God, having explored the vast eras of history and shown us where it is all heading, finally comes back to this: are you getting ready? If you are not, then however much you believe with your head, you can't blame others for saying: "I just don't believe you when you tell me all this, because your life doesn't show it."

8

RAM AND GOAT
Read Daniel 8

A. DANIEL SEES (1–14)
    The vision at Susa (3–14)
        1. Ram
        2. Goat
B. DANIEL SWOONS (15–26)
    The voice of Gabriel (20–26)
        1. Persia
        2. Greece
          a. Alexander the Great
          b. Cassander, Lysimachus,
            Ptolemy, Seleucis
          c. Antiochus Epiphanes
C. DANIEL SICKENS (27)
      1. Israel's sufferings
      2. Israel's sins

GREEK EMPIRE

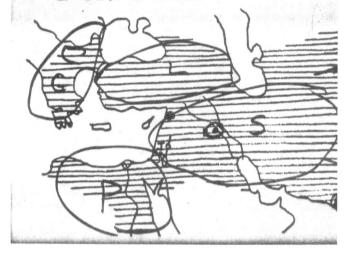

It is fascinating to read predictions about the future. Why don't more people then buy and read the Bible? It is the best book of predictions there is, and certainly the most accurate. Here are some statistics, which I think will impress you. First, twenty-seven percent of the verses of the Bible contain a prediction about future events. So over one-quarter of this book is concerned with the future.

Second, altogether seven hundred and thirty-seven different future events are predicted in detail and I have to tell you now that eighty percent of those predictions have already come true to the letter – so more than four out of every five have been proved right. That does not mean the Bible is only eighty percent correct, because the other fifth are concerned with predictions about the end of the world, and so have yet to occur. But if four out of five have happened, then I think one would be a fool to question the other fifth.

The book of Daniel contains many predictions – in fact forty-five percent of its verses contain a prediction about the future. Most of these are found in chapters seven to twelve, and altogether Daniel predicts fifty-eight separate events, all of which were future in relation to the time of Daniel, and some of them in the distant future too. I want you to imagine that I, David Pawson, dared to make a prediction of an event that would come true in the year 2500 AD or an even later date. That is something that no astrologer or clairvoyant that I know of dares to do (and I certainly don't do this!) but there is a big gap between Daniel and the events which he predicts, events some of which we are seeing in our own lifetimes. Now how can such a thing be? How can you foretell the future like this?

There are only three ways that I know of foretelling the future. There is the human way of forecasting. My brother-in-law was a meteorologist, involved in the business of forecasting. That is why it is a very shaky business. Not because he is my brother-in-law but because he can only use human resources. He can study trends, he can study charts prepared by satellites. He is right sometimes and wrong sometimes. Human forecasting is "guesstimating" and you can only guess what will happen if present trends continue. You can have a think tank. You can have a professor of futurology, as is happening in an increasing number of universities, but they can only guess and they may be right, they may be wrong.

Then we have demonic fortune telling – this is more than forecasting; fortune telling draws on supernatural knowledge of evil spirits. It is more accurate than forecasting and sometimes hits something dead on, but it makes an awful lot of mistakes too, because the practitioners are not all-knowing. Alas, people latch on to the things that are predicted by astrologers and horoscopes and clairvoyants that are accurate, and presume that therefore they are to be trusted. Our world is going crazy trusting such things at the moment.

Then, thirdly, there is divine foretelling. What a difference between human forecasting, satanic fortune telling and divine foretelling. When God predicts, he is always one hundred percent accurate. It doesn't matter how many hundreds of years ahead his predictions may stretch, they always come true in detail, because God is all-knowing. Only he is capable of telling us what will happen next week.

Here is what I think is a very minor demonstration of how he knows the future. I had never taken a congregation through the book of Daniel before I taught on it. Yet God told me eighteen months beforehand to start reading and preparing and studying for it. I had no idea then that every chapter would take on a particular significance because the entire world would be looking at the Middle East during the few weeks when I taught the series. I believe God wanted us to study this book. It was his way of preparing us for what lay ahead.

In chapter eight, Daniel is "dreaming" again, but this time he is daydreaming – his eyes are open, he is awake. He is having a surprising vision. He is still in the capital city of Babylon. That is where he lived, that is where he spent his life from the age of sixteen, having been deported from Jerusalem as a teenager. We have seen that, as an exile from his own land, he rose very high in the court of Nebuchadnezzar, who then died and was replaced by one king after another who was assassinated, until now the reigning monarch is the playboy prince Belshazzar who will lose the entire kingdom in a drunken night of an orgy.

Daniel is worried about the future – the kingdom that he has lived in. The stability of Babylon formerly under the might of Nebuchadnezzar is disintegrating, and he realises this playboy ruler will lose the kingdom, and he is worried about what is happening next. In chapter seven, we saw that in the very first year of Belshazzar God gave him a dream which revealed the ultimate course of human history and the very end of our civilisation. But this chapter, the second vision two years later, is about the immediate future that is going to follow the fall of Babylon. It is going to describe the next three or four hundred years and what will happen to God's people during that time. Very significantly, as we shall see later, Daniel changes his language at this point, and from writing the Chaldean language of Babylon, he now writes this dream in Hebrew so it is locked up for his own people to study. It is about Israel's place over the next three or four hundred years BC.

Funnily enough, in the vision Daniel blinks and looks

around – he is not in Babylon. He is in another town, not in the flesh but in a vision. He is transported one hundred and fifty miles or so due east of Babylon. It is a town in what is now Iran, known today as Shush. Just outside the modern town there you can find the mounds which archeologists have dug up of ancient Susa. In Daniel's day it was a little town of no importance, by a canal joining two rivers. To his surprise, Daniel sees a mighty palace, a fortress, and a capital city at Susa. It is strange that this little canal town is now a capital.

Daniel was not to know that this was to be the summer residence of the kings of Persia, the next empire after Babylon. This was to be the very palace where Esther became the queen. This was to be the very palace where Nehemiah was to be the king's cupbearer. This was to be the palace of Darius and Cyrus and the great kings yet to come, but Daniel was not to know. So he stood by the canal and he wondered what would happen next in the vision. The next thing he saw was a series of animals.

First of all, he saw a two-horned ram, a very familiar beast in that part of the world, tough, strong – they have to be in the conditions in which they live. He saw this powerful ram butting in three directions. He saw it butting in the north direction, west, and south, and nothing could stand before it. It grew great and strong. He saw it rushing across his horizon from east to west. He thought this animal would go on forever until he saw coming from the opposite direction a goat with one large horn – almost a unicorn. This goat came charging from the west towards the east, and they met, and the goat proved the stronger.

Goats are stronger than sheep on the whole. They are tougher, they are often left out on the hills of the Middle East at night. When the sheep are brought in every night, the shepherd separates the sheep from the goats and puts the sheep inside, leaving the goats outside. In the vision, the goat destroys the ram, and the goat gets very strong and grows, and it goes so quickly that its feet don't touch the ground – it literally flies over the ground. Then, at the peak of its power, the horn snaps inexplicably. In place of the single horn there come up four horns – one to the north, one to the west, one to the south, one to the east. Then, as Daniel watches, from one of those horns there comes a little budding horn, which gets big and strong and fierce and is the worst of them all. To his astonishment, the goat turns around, goes back to the west, and that little horn on the goat goes straight for the temple at Jerusalem, does terrible things to the holy city, and Daniel suddenly finds himself in a cold sweat.

What is it all about? He doesn't understand it one bit. Having seen the goat destroy the ram and then depart back to the west he is standing by the canal in his vision and he sees a man coming towards him (or what he thinks is a man), and he hears a loud voice: "Gabriel, tell Daniel what this dream is all about." He knows the figure of a man coming towards him is an angel, a messenger of God. It is the only book in the Old Testament where angels are named.

The word "Gabriel" means "man of God". *Gaber* means man, and *el* means God. So Gabriel, a man of God – the same angel who, centuries later, went to a little teenage girl in Nazareth and said: "You're going to have a baby and it will be the Son of God". This is the same angel that warned Joseph to go to Egypt. There are only two angels with names in the Bible: Gabriel and Michael. They both end with "el", so they are both named after God – God's chief messengers.

Are you looking forward to meeting Gabriel? I tell you what, if he came towards you now you would have the same reactions Daniel had. As this angel moved toward him, Daniel fell on the ground. When the angel began to speak and said, "Daniel, I've come to tell you what it's all about,

I've come to show you the future," Daniel literally fainted. Daniel was a strong man, in his seventies by now, but he swooned, clean away. The angel lifted him on his feet and said, "Daniel, listen, I'm going to tell you what the vision is all about."

So we are going to study it now. Let us listen now to the voice of Gabriel. What were these two animals? What did they mean? We are seeing, in fact, the fulfilment of part of chapter two. Let me take you back to chapter two in Daniel's interpretation of Nebuchadnezzar's dream. Remember, that dream was of a great giant, a warrior who had rather extraordinary clothes. As your eyes travelled down from head to foot he seemed to change. In this gigantic figure, God was showing to Nebuchadnezzar the progression of human civilisation downwards to its doom. The head, which was of gold, was Nebuchadnezzar himself. He was to be followed by the nation or the empire of the Medes and the Persians, together forming the second empire of the Middle East. These were to be followed by the Grecian empire which for another hundred and fifty years would dominate the Middle East; and ultimately there was the Roman power. We saw how things declined as they went down. Now the angel Gabriel says very simply: the ram that you saw is God's understanding of that second empire; it is the symbol of Persia. What you see the ram do, Persia will do. The goat you saw is in fact the symbol of Greece, and what you see the goat do, Greece will do, and that is the simple meaning. So in fact, we are seeing, as it were, the middle part of the image of chapter two expanded in detail, so that Daniel is able to tell his fellow countrymen exactly what is going to happen in the future.

Let us look first at the Persian empire, the ram. You may be familiar with the symbol of the ram as a regimental mascot. Have you ever seen some of our British soldiers walking along with a ram covered with the regimental colours? Did you know that Persia chose the ram for its symbol? Daniel didn't know that when he had this vision, but in fact the ram's head is the symbol of Persia. One reason is that Persia is under the zodiac sign of Aries the ram, and in those days they studied the stars. So Aries the ram is the sign of Persia. More than that, if you go to Persepolis today, that capital city of the Persian King Xerxes, you see on the ruined columns ram sculptures all over the place. Furthermore, when the Persian king went into battle, he wore a ram's head on his head to lead his troops. In other words: come on, we are going to deal with these people. The two horns out of his forehead represented invincible power. The two horns' clear meaning is that one is larger than the other and grows stronger.

The Persians ultimately became the dominant partner in the empire, and so we now call it the empire of Persia. The Medes were included. The conquests of this Persia starting in what is modern Iran were: to the north, into Armenia, Afghanistan, central Russia; to the west as far as the end of what we now call Turkey; and to the south, way down the Nile into Egypt, the very three directions that we are told about. This Persian Empire lasted two hundred years.

They did what they wished. They spread throughout the Middle East, but they did one thing that was to be remembered and avenged a hundred and fifty years later: they crossed into Europe. They did not occupy it, they raided the colonies of Greece. They devastated them with great cruelty. The few survivors of those scattered Greek colonies never forgot and never forgave. Deep within their subconscious ambition was a desire to get their own back on Persia, and we are going to see that they did.

For two hundred years this empire, larger than the empire of Babylon, dominated the Middle East. Susa – here was the new capital, a hundred and fifty miles east across the

Tigris and the Euphrates. But they dominated the Holy Land including Jerusalem, the Nile, the whole lot. In the twentieth century, the Shah of Persia said when interviewed that it was his intention to revive the Persian empire of two thousand five hundred years earlier. As we know, Iran became a major power in the Middle East in modern times. Before his overthrow, the Shah of Persia reclaimed the title of Darius. He crowned himself and his queen and took to himself the title "king of kings". It was his declared intention to be that ram again. So we are talking about the modern era, not ancient history. So the ram was not totally extinct, but what happened to it in those days? Why did it shrink? The answer you know already: the Greek empire came. Now why should a goat be the symbol of Greece? Again, bear in mind that now Daniel is thinking over two hundred years ahead, and he says that goat will come. Did you know that the goat is the symbol of Greece? Did you know that on the ruins of Macedonian monuments you still see the goat? Do you know why? It was because when the first Greek colony was founded, a priest prophesied that a herd of goats would lead them to the place of that first colony. They followed a herd of goats and they were led to the area around what we now call Edessa. There they founded the colony and they called it Goat City. They called the sea next to it the Aegean Sea – the Goat's Sea, and it is still called that. Did you know that the leaders, the kings of Greece and Macedonia, wore horns pointing out from their heads? If you look at coins of those kings, you will see the horns sticking out of their hair at the sides. Now let us look into the meaning of this. Who is the goat with one horn? Who is this big horn that is going to challenge the Persian Empire and defeat it?

The answer is very simple to us in the light of history. Daniel didn't know, but we know. It was Alexander the Great. His life history is fascinating. He was born to Philip II of Macedonia, an ambitious father who trained his son in feats of skill and strength and got him the best education. Aristotle was his tutor—the difficulty was that his mother was a violent, immoral woman, and she passed on her violent passion to her son. This boy Alexander grew up. He watched his father and warriors trying to break in a wild horse and they all failed. The boy said, "Let me try," and he turned the horse toward the sun so the horse could no longer see its shadow, and he tamed the horse. His father cried out, "Search out a kingdom for yourself, for Macedonia is not going to be big enough for you."

This planted a seed in little Alexander's mind. That thought grew so much that it became an obsession with him. He must have the biggest empire that the world had seen. Whenever his father conquered new territory, the boy would burst into tears and say, "Father is leaving me nothing to do." When Alexander was twenty, his father died and Alexander swore that he would avenge the Persians who, a hundred and fifty years earlier, had ravaged the Greek colonies. He went to the oracle at Delphi to consult the priestess about his fortune. He was told he had come on the wrong day. It was the priestess's half day, and she wasn't prophesying that day. I am telling you the truth – this is not imagination. Brushing aside the priests, he seized the priestess, dragged her into the temple and said, "Prophesy." Understandably, she said, "Alexander you are invincible," and equally understandably he said, "That is all I wanted."

So it was that – his father having died or been assassinated – he set off from his home palace with twenty thousand infantry and five thousand cavalry to conquer the world. He steered his own boat across to Troy, the scene of his greatest hero, the scene of the greatest battle. He slept with Homer's *Iliad* under his pillow and he was always reading the story of the battle of Troy. Into Troy he came, and he took the city.

He took the sacred shield into the temple of Troy, a shield that saved his life eight years later. Then he set off to what we now call Turkey.

Down through Lebanon, through to Israel, he went into Jerusalem. He took Jerusalem. The high priest refused to pay him tax, but Alexander didn't kill him. He bowed down and worshipped him because, he said, "Last night I had a dream and I saw the clothes that you wear, and I believe your God is real" – and he sacrificed to Yahweh. The high priest of Jerusalem took the book of Daniel and showed it to him and said, "The book of Daniel says a Greek would conquer Persia," and Alexander replied, "I'm that Greek." He went down and down – to Egypt. He founded a city called after his own name, and it is still there: Alexandria.

While his architects were laying it out for him he took botanists, surveyors, architects, all sorts of people, with him and he went right out into Almena, in the desert. It was not called that then. He went out to consult a pagan priest of the god Amon, the horned god. The pagan priest said, "The world is yours." From then on, Alexander always wore the horns of Amon on his head when he went into battle. Back up through Jordan, back up through Syria, chasing back Darius's army. Even though by this time Alexander had about thirty-five thousand men in his army, Darius had one million. Yet at each of three major battles Alexander outflanked him. Surprise, speed – his strategy was superb. On to the east, on through what is now Iraq. When he came to a great river he made his troops stuff their tents with straw and float across the river on them. He took them over twelve thousand foot-high mountain passes in thick snow. He took them through the famous desert of death and they were dropping on all sides, and he marched on thirty-five thousand miles on foot in eleven years, and he conquered one and a half million square miles – an area bigger than the United States today.

Alexander became a legend in his own lifetime – the Great.

Finally, he defeated the Persians. Darius the king of Persia said, "Look I'll give you my daughter. I'll give you ten million pounds' worth of gold" [that is expressed in our terms]. "I will give you a third of the kingdom if you will sign a peace treaty." So Alexander asked his military advisor, Parmenion, "What would you do?"

Parmenion said, "If I were Alexander I would accept the offer."

Alexander replied, "If I were Parmenion I would, but I'm Alexander." He defeated Darius, outflanking a million men. On, on he went, came to Babylon, Susa, went on, up into Armenia, up into Russia, out into Afghanistan, down to Pakistan, into India, across the Indus River and under cover of a thunderstorm when the people thought he would never go, on he went. The world was his and he was still only in his late twenties. What a man – the horned goat, this buck who flew so fast that he conquered five major cities in two days. His feet didn't touch the ground. How true the scripture is, and the scripture said something else about Alexander as it does about all human aggressors: the horn will be broken.

When he got to India, the troops began to mutiny. They were homesick, they were weary. He was too. He had had an arrow through his lungs. He was an old man already in his late twenties/early thirties, but he struggled on; he was determined. You see, he had one great rival – himself. He always had to beat himself. But there came the crisis in India when his troops mutinied, and the general came and said, "We must go back," and to Alexander: "It is a noble thing to know when to stop." Alexander sulked for three days in his tent, weeping that he could not conquer more. Then he gave in because he realised the troops were determined to go home.

So he turned back and the army said forever afterwards,

"Alexander allowed us but no one else to defeat him," and they slowly came back. They came back to Susa, remember, and there ten thousand of his troops married ten thousand Persian women and he married Barsine. He had already married Roxanna and Barsine was another Persian woman. An interesting thing happened at Susa. They brought back from India a fortune teller, a fakir. This Indian fakir died at Susa and as he died he said to Alexander, "Alexander, we shall meet again in Babylon."

They pressed back to Babylon and there at last his way of living caught up with him. He was now an alcoholic. He was drinking heavily. He was losing his temper. He had killed even the man who had saved his life in battle, and he was rapidly going to pieces. His pace of living had been too much. At Babylon he became ill of a fever. He was paralysed and speechless. Every officer in the army came to his tent and he managed to salute everyone with a nod of his head, but Alexander was finished. At thirty-two years of age the horn was broken and Alexander was done. So runs the story of Alexander the Great.

Even in the twentieth century in Afghanistan they played a game of polo. There were men on horseback who were direct descendants of those who fiercely fought Alexander. They are playing a game called Buzkashi. That name of that game means "dead goat", for they play not with a ball but with the body of a dead goat. They will tell you the game is centuries old. They cannot trace the origin but I will tell you what I believe to be the origin: the dead goat, and it survives in that kind of folklore.

When Alexander died, his kingdom was divided up between four generals. One general took the north, one took the west, one took the south, and one the east: Cassander, Lysimachus, Ptolemy, and the key one we're going to look at in just a moment, Seleucus. The four horns came true and the kingdom broke up after just eleven years. Cassander was the general who took the west, Ptolemy took the south. Licinius took another area, and the eastern part was taken over by Seleucus.

From that fourth horn, Seleucus, there came one day a new-looking horn who was to be the worst enemy of Israel in the whole of the Old Testament. His name is preserved in the capital city Antioch, for his name was Antiochus and it is still there in what is now Syria. Incidentally, Babylon is where Alexander the Great died. It is with the little horn Antiochus that we are now concerned – the worst of the bunch. We are now out of the period of the Old Testament. I am sure you know that between the Old and the New Testament is a period of four hundred years, a gap between Malachi and Matthew. There were historical records kept during that period and we call the books that were written in that time the Apocrypha. If you want to read about Antiochus and the dreadful things he did you must read the books called the first and second books of Maccabees, for his doings are described there.

So this man forecasted in Daniel's vision came horribly true. He was cunning, he was fierce, he was deceitful, he would actually send a peace representative to discuss a truce to keep his enemies occupied while he brought his troops in another way—that is the kind of man he was. It says in Daniel 8 he turned his attention to the east. It says he turned his attention south to Egypt, but it says he also turned to the pleasant or beautiful land. What land was that? – Israel.

He made the biggest mistake of his career, as so many have done, by turning against Israel. We have many mixed thoughts today about the British attitude to Israel. I feel uncomfortable to say the least that we were prepared in 1939 to go to the rescue of a nation that had been attacked but now we want to keep out of trouble. I wonder what would have been our attitude if a major part of our energy resources had not been at stake.

The nation that takes a stand against Israel faces doom. Hitler didn't realise that in the 1930s. The worst thing he ever did was not to invade Poland but to attack the Jews, and Antiochus did just this. What I have to tell you of what he did is horrible. He invaded Jerusalem, he deposed Onias the high priest, putting in his own puppet priest. He destroyed the altars of God. He built his own altar in the temple of God in Jerusalem – in the city of God – to Zeus (also known as Jupiter). It is significant that the statue of Zeus had the face of Antiochus on it. Not only that, but he took pigs, the unclean animal of Israel, and offered them on the altar—pork on the altar in the temple in the city of God. He profaned everything he touched. He said, "You must profane the Sabbath on pain of death." When they refused, he slaughtered forty thousand Jews in three days and deported ten thousand as slaves in chains. This is what Antiochus did – he set himself against the God of Israel and he took for himself the title "Epiphanes", the same as our word "epiphany". It means glorious, shining, and it is a title of God. His enemies changed one letter and said Antiochus Epimenides, which means Antiochus the maniac. He made life more and more intolerable for faithful Jews.

Now all this was in Daniel's vision three or four hundred years earlier. In the vision Daniel heard two angels chatting and one said, "How long is that going to go on?" The other angel said, "Two thousand three hundred days." What an extraordinary prediction, but let me tell you now that it was in the year 171 BC that Antiochus deposed Onias the high priest as the first act of sacrilege against the God of Israel, and he died in the year 165 BC—exactly two thousand three hundred days later. Isn't the Word of God remarkable? That was said three or four hundred years previously, and Antiochus Epiphanes died. It said in Daniel 8 that he would be broken without a man's hand. Do you know what happened to Antiochus? He was in the middle of a battle and he was stricken with physical colic and manic depression. The two were too much and he perished. No man's hand killed this dreadful beast of a man.

He was the worst enemy Israel ever had – he nearly stamped out Judaism. He almost succeeded in ending the religion of the Jews before Jesus their Messiah came. What stopped him? One faithful priest and his five sons stopped him. They were the Maccabees family. That priest and his sons led a courageous and heroic stand against this man Antiochus Epiphanes and they won. Judaism was restored and the temple was cleansed. Isn't that marvellous? Centuries later, the composer Handel was so struck by this account that he wrote the oratorio *Judas Maccabeus* at the request of the Prince of Wales.

As Daniel was told this, it is said he felt ill. Do these things not make you feel ill? When Daniel realised something, he felt sick for days. Why? Some people have thought that he was ill because of the vision of Israel's future suffering. You see, this was in Jerusalem and he realised that Israel would be back in her own land. They thought that once they got back from Babylon into Jerusalem and rebuilt the temple, that they were safe. Now he realised that Israel back in her own land is not safe – doesn't that make you feel sick? This is the feeling we have got now – that Israel is in her own land and is not safe. But is this the only reason that Israel was going to suffer after she got back – that under the Greeks Israel would go through the desecration of her own temple? No, there was something worse that made Daniel sick. It is just a little hint in the chapter. Why should a good God allow Israel to get back to her own temple and then let that happen? The answer in Daniel 8 is this: it is

God's indignation against Israel's transgression – that is what makes him sick. History bears out Daniel 8 here. How was Antiochus able to get into Jerusalem? Because Greek culture had been accepted by the people of God long before he got there. This is the tragedy of it all. They had stopped reading their Hebrew scriptures, and they were reading Greek philosophers. They had stopped using Hebrew names, Bible names for their children and they were using Greek names because they were the fashion. They had stopped wearing their own clothes; they were wearing Greek clothes. Everything was going Greek, even the entertainment was going Greek in Jerusalem, long before Antiochus got there. They had built a vast gymnasium in Jerusalem itself where they had Greek sports – nothing wrong with sport, though we are told in the New Testament bodily exercise profits little but godliness is something much better than that. Having said that, you see what was wrong with Greek sports: they were always performed in total nudity, and nudity had never been seen in Jerusalem before this but now it was part of the entertainment. The Greek culture was filtering right through Jerusalem. Can you imagine it?

The truth is that when Antiochus came he found a Greek city. He had found a city that had already accepted his ways, his language, his dress, his entertainment – the lot. All he needed to do was walk in and take over and say, "You've already accepted me." The tragedy is, and here I tremble, it was the clergy that had led them in this direction, apart from the Maccabean priest. It was the clergy who were preaching Greek philosophy from the pulpit instead of Hebrew scripture. It was those who should have been leading the men, the people of God, in the right way who were misleading them. Do you see the relevance of all this to today? So Antiochus walked in and Daniel felt sick that he had done it because of Israel's transgressions. God had said: My people have accepted Greece already so let them have a Greek leader. It is tragic. It took all Daniel's courage to pull himself together and get on with the king's business.

Have we exhausted the meaning of Daniel 8 when we have mentioned Antiochus? No, because Daniel is told by the angels that these are things that will take place in the end of the times. Does this have a deeper meaning? Is there something in Daniel 8 that even points to our future and not just our past? Is there a fulfilment yet waiting to be seen? I believe there is, and that Antiochus himself is not the total fulfilment of this vision. Have you noticed that there is a link between chapter eight and chapter seven? Go back to the previous chapter. Do you remember that final ghastly beast we saw? Let me remind you of it. Do you remember that ten horns came up on its head, and the little horn that came up after them replaced three and became the world's last dictator, Antichrist? The things said about Antichrist in chapter 7 are the same things said about Antiochus in chapter 8. Therefore, I am going to point out now something that I hope will help you to see what this means. Antiochus was the antichrist of the Old Testament and foreshadowed (and was an example of) the Antichrist of the New who has yet to appear on the world scene. What Antiochus did to Israel, some future world dictator will do to the people of God, including us. As I see that, I suddenly see Daniel 8 in a new light. Their names are even similar sounding. Antiochus, Antichrist – yes, there is something here that points very much to the future. Jesus himself is our warrant for using what is said about Antiochus to understand what is going to happen with Antichrist.

Let me give you one example: when Antiochus built that horrible altar and put pork on it, and burnt pork in front of Yahweh's face, they said, "He has put the abomination of desolation where it ought not to be." Jesus, in his last week on earth, said to his disciples, "When you see the abomination of desolation where it ought not to be, then you know that the end is getting near." Oh, this makes me sick – to think that we have got to go through all this again before our Lord Jesus returns. As Antiochus came and polluted that temple, the Lord Jesus came and cleansed it just before he spoke those words about the abomination of desolation. So I come to the most challenging and stirring question of all: are you getting ready for Christ or Antichrist?

Let me tell you this: when Antichrist comes, when the evil dictator who is to head up the whole of our world at the end of human affairs comes, the tragedy is he will find that the people, often the people of God, have already accepted his culture and are waiting for him to take over. God will just be saying: you have already accepted his culture then you can have him. Insofar as we adopt the philosophy, the entertainment, the dress, the fashions of Satan, we cannot blame God for allowing Satan to be the king of this world. This is the meaning of Daniel chapter 8 for us. The Jews have always been an example of the danger of assimilation. Orthodox Jews who stay with the faith of their fathers are regarded as old-fashioned, narrow-minded and out of date. The other Jews assimilate to their surroundings and become like other people.

In the same way, the people of God can do the same thing, and I confess with shame that it has often been us clergy who have preached Greek philosophy from the pulpit rather than the Hebrew scriptures. That is the tragedy of our day, and so the culture of Antichrist is already with us, and insofar as we accept the standards of the world, the behaviour of the world, the ideas of the world and the teaching of the world, we are preparing for the coming of Antichrist. But insofar as we remain faithful to God, whether we be called old-fashioned or narrow-minded, we are preparing for the coming of Christ and we are making it possible for him to say to us one day, "Well done, good and faithful servant." That doesn't make me sick, that makes me feel very well – that Christ is coming.

We have shared in Daniel's vision, we have seen things you may never have looked at before, and it is our world but it is God's world basically. Satan only does what God allows him to do, and one day all things are to be put right, and the aggressive powers of the Middle East and the whole world, and those who have butted in every direction, and those who have overrun and trampled nations, and those who have turned against Israel – all will bow down before our God, Yahweh, the Father of Jesus, and acknowledge that Jesus Christ is Lord to the glory of God the Father.

9

SEVENTY SEVENS
Read Daniel 9

A. PROMISE OF SCRIPTURE (1–2)
    1. When? Darius the Mede's first year
    2. What? Seventy years to first return
B. PRAYER OF SUPPLICATION (3–19)
    1. Why? Jehovah righteous; Judah rebellious
    2. What? Judah derided; Jehovah despised
C. PROPHECY OF SALVATION (20–27)
    1. Who? Gabriel's swift answer
    2. What? 70 x 7 years to restoration
        a. 70 weeks = 490 years (24)
          i. Rebelliousness ended
          ii. Righteousness established
        b. 69 weeks = 483 years (25)
          i. Principality rebuilt
          ii. Prince received
        c. "After" 62 weeks (26)
          i. Jesus crucified
          ii. Jerusalem crushed
        d. Last week = 70 years
          i. Pact enforced
          ii. Persecution entailed

In the *New York Herald Tribune* some years ago there appeared a cartoon which showed an elderly American sitting in a chair reading that newspaper. The headline was: "Israel Declared a State." A little boy playing on the floor at the feet of his grandfather was saying, "Grandpa, now that Israel is back in her own land, what will happen next?" The grandfather is replying, "Hold on while I get my Bible." To many people this is the strangest thing to do. They imagine that if you want to know what is happening in our world, the meaning and significance of contemporary events, you have to read newspapers. But newspapers are severely limited in what they can tell you. They can tell you the immediate past and present, but that is far too narrow a view to understand what is happening in our world.

The Bible is far more relevant. More people, instead of reading their newspapers on the train to London should read their Bible and really find out what is happening in our situation, and to our nation – for it is all there. Daniel is one of those books in the Bible that are a mixture of history and prophecy. History is a record of the past; prophecy is often a record of the future. History in the Bible is usually dated very carefully.

In Daniel chapter 9 we have the miracle of God actually enabling people to describe what will happen, and not only what will happen but when it will happen – to the year, and up to five centuries ahead. Only God can produce the miracle of prophecy and write the history of events five hundred years before they occur. Now we are going to look very deeply into this chapter. We start with the *promise of scripture*. It all began when Daniel, as a man of eighty-seven, read the scriptures. We will never get too old to read our Bibles. An old lady who was reading the Bible was asked, "Why are you doing it at your age?" She replied, "I am swotting for my finals!" Daniel at eighty-seven is still a Bible student. He still prefers God's Word to other writings. So he is reading God's Word, and he is reading because of the days in which he lived. He was reading it in the first year of Darius reigning over conquered Babylon.

What is he looking for? He is looking for some clue to the meaning in God's plan of the change that has taken place in the country he has known since his teens. Babylon has fallen. The last King, Belshazzar, has held that drunken orgy and is dead. Now the Persians have conquered, and Cyrus the King of Persia has put his nephew Darius in as viceroy of Babylon. Daniel is chief minister of state again, and, thankfully, Daniel is not the kind of politician who has no time for God's Word – he reads the scriptures.

The question in his mind is this: how is the change in government going to affect God's people? Now that we are under the Persians, is there a chance of us getting back to our own land – to the freedom we once enjoyed? Does the change in government mean liberation for us? It was a natural question for it was the cruel tyrant Nebuchadnezzar who had dragged the young Daniel away from his home, as well as hundreds of his fellow countrymen, and ultimately, only a few years later, destroyed Jerusalem, razing it to the ground. Will this new government mean liberty? He goes to God with this question before he asks Darius the new king, or Cyrus the new emperor. Though Cyrus is going to be the one to give them their liberty, Daniel goes to God and says, "God, what do you say? What's next in your plan?" Before he prays he studies God's Word. How important it is to listen to what God has already said before we ask him to say something more. God has already said thousands of things to us, and our first job is to find out what he has already said and then to ask him, "Have you any more enlightenment to give us in addition to what we have read?"

Of course, Daniel did not have all the Bible we have. He didn't have the New Testament; he didn't have all the Old Testament – he was still writing part of it in his own bedside diary – but he had books in which were recorded the words of God to previous prophets, among them a man whom he had known as a teenager when he was in Jerusalem, a lonely man called Jeremiah. Of all the preachers in Israel at that time, Jeremiah had been the one who had prophesied doom and they called him a pessimist. To this day, if you are pessimistic people might call you a "Jeremiah".

When the other prophets said "peace", Jeremiah said "war". When the other prophets said "security", Jeremiah said "exile". Even when the exile happened and the first few thousand people were taken away in chains, the false preacher said, "It will only be a couple of years." But Jeremiah said, "It will be seventy years before they get back." Jeremiah was not a popular preacher. He didn't comfort people and send them away feeling so nice after a lovely sermon. He left them hating him because he disturbed their peace and security so deeply.

But Jeremiah knew that nothing God does is arbitrary. He knew that the land had to be empty, desolate – for seventy years. Do you know why? There is a very simple and obvious reason, and as a former farmer, I appreciate the reason. God had told them: you can have this Holy Land, but you must look after it; therefore, every seventh year you must give the land a sabbatical rest and it must lie fallow one year in seven. For four hundred and ninety years they had not allowed the land to be fallow. The greedy agriculturists had been taking crop after crop after crop, only interested in making money. They were doing the kind of thing that is done in agriculture today, believing that you can go on treating God's land with greed without any fear of comeback.

God said that his land must lie fallow for seventy years and have its sabbatical, that is how it worked out. You will find it clearly put in Chronicles. For four hundred and ninety years they had been so greedy that they would not give the holy land of God its seventh rest. So God arranged that it was rested for seventy years and then they could come back. When God decides a period of time, there is a reason for it – always. He is not arbitrary.

So Daniel, reading through the book of Jeremiah, is trying to find the answer to this question: when will we get back into our own land and into our own city? His heart must have missed a beat when he read "seventy years" because he has already been away just over sixty-seven years. Now in his eighties, maybe he wondered if he would live to see it. He knows that it is nearly here. So the old man reading Jeremiah gets the answer.

It is in Jeremiah chapters 25 and 29. If you read chapter 29 carefully you will see that connected to this promise of return to Jerusalem is a condition. The condition is: *If you seek me with your whole heart you will find me and I will hear you and answer you.* In other words, this will not happen automatically. Prayer is needed. After seventy years, when you call upon me, you'll find me and I'll hear and I'll end your slavery.

Daniel realises in a flash that nearly seventy years have gone and they are in sight of the possibility of going back, and no one is praying. That is the amazing discovery that he makes and what turns his whole life upside down at this point. They could go back if they called, but they are not calling. So Daniel didn't make the mistake some Christians make and blame everybody else for not praying and for not doing what God had told them to do. Daniel says, "I'll start." Quite deliberately, he prepared in a determined way to pray for the fulfilment of that promise of God. He set his face to

God. There is something determined about that. He realised that all the pomp of his Prime Minister's robes were unfitting for the prayer he had to pray, so he changed his clothes, put on sackcloth and ashes, and he went without his meal and sought God's face.

The idea that you should pray only when you feel like it, when you are nice and bouncy, is far removed from this. To Daniel, prayer was hard work. He rolled up his sleeves for it and got down to it. Someone has got to pray to God that this promise may be fulfilled. Someone has got to get us back to Jerusalem; the seventy years are nearly up. He lived to see the first return, though he himself never got back.

So we turn to the promise of scripture – to the prayer of supplication. What a prayer! It teaches us many tremendous lessons; it is a model in praying for the nation.

We, no less than Israel, are getting exactly what we deserve. The only thing is that we are not getting all that we deserve *yet*. We are an unchristian nation. If ever anybody taught us how to pray for our own nation, it is Daniel in this prayer. Let us see what we can learn from it.

We notice he begins with worship and adoration and praise for what God is and does. This note of worship keeps coming in all the way through. He keeps making lovely statements about how wonderful God is. We must always pray against that backcloth. The God who is loyal, the God who keeps his Word, the God who is merciful, the God who delivers his people with a mighty hand—again and again, Daniel turns to how wonderful God is; it is always the note of praise creeping through. But I want you to note that he says "sorry" before he says "please", and here is the great secret of the prayer that God loves to hear. Natural man comes into God's presence with a shopping list: "Please this, please that, please the other." But the spiritual man comes into God's presence with "Sorry for this, sorry for that, sorry for the other." As he has read Jeremiah, the whole horror of the situation has dawned on Daniel, and the enormity of the guilt of his nation is clearly seen. God had been so good to them. He had brought them out of Egypt, he had given them their own land, he had given them his laws; he had given them verbal warnings and written warnings that if they did not use his land properly they would lose it. He sent prophet after prophet after prophet and they took no notice whatever. They waited till the prophets were dead and then they put up monuments to them. I think of that every time I see the bronze statue of Charles Haddon Spurgeon in the Baptist Union headquarters.

This is what we do to the voices of the Lord; we force them out while they are alive and we put up a statue to them when they are dead. That is what they did to the prophets, and Daniel sees this unfolding. He suddenly sees sin for what it is and he now uses the very strongest words in the Hebrew language to describe what they have done. He says, "We've sinned, we've missed the mark. We have been traitors, we're bent." That's the literal word he uses in the Hebrew: "we're bent" – and he piles up the language. Every word is the strongest word he can use. How feeble our own English synonyms for sin sound. We talk about our "faults", our "failings" and our "weaknesses". But Daniel says we have been *traitors*. Our very restlessness shows what we have been, and he pours it all out, because though God has been so good to them, they had been so bad to him.

It had been right through the nation. It is the easiest thing to single out one little group in a nation and say they are to blame. That political party is the cause of all our problems. It is this lot! If we could get this lot in and this lot out, we would be alright. We blame the government, we blame the trade unions, we blame mass media; we blame everybody. But Daniel says of his people that it is right through – our kings, our princes, our people, the lot; we are all in it together. Therefore, in our time there is no call for any of us to point at anyone else and say they are to blame for the mess the nation is in.

So Daniel confesses it and says the catastrophe that happened was utterly deserved. "Oh God, you are fair in everything you do and you had a perfect right to smash our land and our city. Lord, I'm not grumbling about that; you were absolutely right to do it." But I want you to notice something that Daniel does: he never uses the word "them". That is all the more remarkable because when these things had happened Daniel was just a baby, and he could have said, "Well, I wasn't alive when they did it; I have been in exile all my adult responsible life. I was just a boy, so I had nothing to do with it." He could truly point to the fact that he had lived a godly life.

There are only two people in the Old Testament of whom no sin is ever recorded. Both of them became prime ministers in exile: Joseph and Daniel. Not even his enemies could find anything wrong with him. Daniel could have pointed to others: the people who used to live in Jerusalem. But he was too spiritual a man to do that. It takes a holy man to be sensitive to real sin and it takes a holy man to identify with it. So Daniel said "we", "our", "us".

We are going to get nowhere in Britain until we are prepared to pray, "We...." It's no use blaming others. The tragedy is that protest movements always say "them". What Britain is waiting for is not a Christian protest movement but a Christian prayer movement that says "we". Daniel confessed the nation's state.

It was not just a mental posture, he felt it. He felt his own face blush; he was confused himself. He was shamefaced. He sought the Lord's face and then he found he couldn't face him, and he is being utterly honest that he felt he was not being on God's side but on the nation's side, and it was the wrong side. What a prayer!

I was once in a debate at the Baptist Union Council when a minister got up and said, "What can we do to try and stop – legally – old churches being turned into bingo halls and furniture warehouses?" I wanted to cry out, "We can stop that by filling them all." It is our fault because most of those have gone empty because of lack of business and because people don't want to come and pray to God. So we are all in it: church and nation. We have failed our nation, and our nation no longer listens to us because we haven't given them the Word of God. We have given them the comfortable instead of the Comforter.

So we deserve everything we get, and if this country is driven to its knees financially – we deserve it. If we have to walk to church and can't come in our cars, we deserve it. If we have to dig up our flower beds and grow our own vegetables, we deserve it. When you consider what God has done for us in this country: for two thousand years he sent missionaries to us. We have more Bibles in our language than any other language on earth. We have church and chapel buildings able to accommodate meetings in total freedom in every community throughout this land. We have had some of the greatest preachers that the world has seen. We have had everything our way, and we are taking no notice whatever and we just tip our hats to God by holding royal events in Westminster Abbey. Two hundred yards from that same Abbey we pass laws that are absolutely contrary to God's laws. We will not escape. God is fair, God is just, and we deserve as a nation, I believe, to be damned for the opportunities we have had and missed.

Daniel doesn't stop praying there, he goes on praying. He now pleads for mercy – he knows what he wants and he knows how to get it. If you want to learn how to get a prayer answered, listen to Daniel. He knows how he can persuade God. First of all, he presents what he wants to God. He says, "God I want us back in our land. I want you to restore our nation. I want you to get us back in Jerusalem and get it rebuilt; that's what I want. I am asking for that."

You should always be specific in prayer and know what you want to ask for. But you should also be able to present God with some very good reasons for giving it to you. This is the reason why so many of our requests are not answered – we are not able to give God good reasons for doing it, but Daniel is. What, then, are the grounds on which he asks for this to be done? He does not say "on the grounds of our righteousness" – there isn't any. So that is no reason. There is no reason to come to God and say, "I go to church regularly and I try to live decently." This is not good enough.

Daniel says, "God, you're a merciful God, I come for that reason." Well that is a good one, but not enough. Then he comes to God and says, "God, I am going to plead with you on the basis of the promises in your Word." That is a good reason, and if you can find a promise that does fit your condition, you can pray that. But you must not twist it out of its context. Find a promise that really fits your condition, then say, "God, that's your Word, you keep it." That is a good ground for persuading him, but the best ground of all is the one that Daniel keeps on emphasising. He is saying: God, it's your reputation that's at stake; this is your people, your city, and it is your name; the Jews are being derided where we have become a byword, a joke among people. "We have become a taunt among the people." Deuteronomy 28 said they would be just that if they left their God. Daniel is saying: they're laughing at us but, God, it's you they are deriding; it is you they are despising because we are known by your name. It is for God's sake that Daniel prayed this prayer.

Now if you can prove to God that it is for his glory, you

can persuade him to act. You see, most of our requests to God are to gratify ourselves rather than to glorify him. You are to come to God and prove to him that the answer to your prayer is for his sake – not for your comfort, not for your ease, but for his sake.

Daniel pleads: *your* name, *your* sake and *your* glory. So bold and confident is he on this ground that he says to the Lord, "Delay not." He is asking for an immediate answer. You can have a holy boldness in prayer because you have got the grounds for boldness, because you are sure of your ground.

As Daniel prayed, he turned around and the angel Gabriel says, "I've got the answer for you." It's tremendous isn't it? It says, literally, the angel touched him. Here he is saying, "God I want an answer immediately" – and the angel Gabriel is there. He hasn't seen him for ten years. He doesn't fall in terror this time because he recognises what is happening.

We are moving now to the next part of our study: *the prophecy of salvation*. One man's prayer can change a nation's history if that man is a Daniel. A prayer like this from a man like this stirs heaven. The angel Gabriel says, "As soon as you started praying, God told me to come." How is this for swift space flight from highest heaven to Daniel's bedroom before he finished praying? "Daniel, the Lord sent me to tell you how he is going to answer your prayer" – immediate answer! If we prayed like Daniel, from Daniel's character to Daniel's record to Daniel's passion; from Daniel's confession, from Daniel's everything else, maybe we would get immediate answers more frequently than we do.

Gabriel is letting Daniel know that he is beloved ("highly esteemed", NIV). God loves people like this because they are the ones he can cooperate with, the kind he loves to bless. God had already sent the answer and we are going to look at it now – the last four verses of chapter nine. From one point of view Daniel got what he wanted: an immediate answer. From another point of view it was a disappointing answer. The humour of it strikes me a little. Daniel says, "I want an answer soon; now." God is going to answer his prayer but it will take him four hundred and ninety years to do it. Oh what a different perspective God has – how much patience the Lord has with us. We want an answer by Tuesday and God says that he is going to do it in four hundred and ninety years' time. But to God time is so different. A thousand years is like a day, and four hundred and ninety years just a half a day's work to him. We are so much in a hurry and we want God to do it just like that, and God has it all planned.

It says that God has literally cut off and snipped out four hundred and ninety years – to do what Daniel has asked him to do. The word is used of tailors who cut a length of cloth to make a suit. Literally, God said "seventy weeks", but the word "weeks" is not our literal word "week". It means seven. So he says, "seventy sevens". When we read through the predictions and apply them to history there is no doubt what it means. It means "seventy sevens" of years. God was saying about those people who had been getting into a mess for four hundred and ninety years, that he was going to get them out of it in four hundred and ninety years. Who says God isn't fair? Who says God is arbitrary? Can't you see why God plans what he does?

So we are going to look now very briefly at this four hundred and ninety years or seventy "weeks". There has been so much argument over the interpretation of these verses that I can't hope to give you all the interpretations – there are dozens. I am just going to give you the one that seems to me the plainest and simplest, and leave you to study the rest for yourself. But if you just get the impression that God knows what he is doing, that is the main thing.

We can get bogged down in the intellectual exercise of Daniel's seventy weeks. One Old Testament commentator said, "These verses are the dismal swamp of Old Testament critics." Well, that is true. Once you get bogged down in Daniel's seventy weeks you are here for life. Let me point out that Daniel made the simple step of believing the scriptures to be literally true. So when it said "seventy years" he believed it meant seventy years – the simplest way to read your Bible, and he was right.

We make heavy weather of biblical interpretation because we so often do not take literally what is meant to be taken literally. People say to me, "Do you still take the Bible literally?" – as if somehow that really is not the thing to do today with all the scholarship about. Some say that we must try to find some peculiar hidden meaning in it, but it is a simple principle of Bible study that you believe it in its simple sense unless some other part of the Bible tells you not to.

So Daniel said, "seventy years" – that means seventy years. And he looked for the answer, and he was right. So when the scripture says another four hundred and ninety years, I take it as another four hundred and ninety years, and we will see that is right. So take the Bible literally. God didn't want to confuse us, he didn't want to hide the truth from us; he wants to talk to you, and so he puts it in its simple, plain sense.

Let me take these four verses as simply and plainly as I can. In the first verse, God is saying that he has snipped four hundred and ninety years out of time to deal with Israel. But then there is more. The message from God now announced by Gabriel means: Daniel, do you realise that you are not asking for the total solution to the problem? You are just asking that Israel may be forgiven and the penalty of her sin removed – I want to remove the power of sin; I want to get them righteous.

That is so often what we pray for. We say, "Lord, forgive me." We don't realise that not only does the Lord want to forgive it; he wants to remove it. So he not only wants to end sin and take away transgression and make atonement for iniquity, he wants to establish righteousness. He wants to seal up the visions and the prophets by fulfilling them and finishing them and putting them away in the cupboard so that these predictions are no longer needed. He wants to anoint the Holy of holies and he wants to have a holy shrine among his people.

So in verse twenty-four God is saying: It will take me four hundred and ninety years, seventy weeks of years, seventy times seven years; the same length of time you got into the mess, it will take me that to get you out of it to the point where your sin goes; you are undergoing a moral transformation and you will never do again the things that lost you the city.

You see, this is still not true of Israel today. Israel is still sinning and that is why she is still in difficulties in the Holy Land.

So God is saying: I'm going to complete the job – negatively an end to sin and atonement for iniquity and taking away transgressions; positively, to establish everlasting righteousness, to make you good. Not only to forget the penalty and put you back in Jerusalem, but to remove the power of sin and have you there as a righteous people. It will take me four hundred and ninety years to get you like that. So that is the first verse. Now the second verse, twenty-five. God talks about the first sixty-nine weeks of years, or four hundred and eighty years. From God's total strategy we now move to his tactics. How is he going to do it?

Well, pay attention very carefully now. In the first sixty-nine weeks, two things will be accomplished. First of all, in the first forty-nine years – that is the first seven weeks of seven years (just over one generation), Jerusalem will be rebuilt. That is exactly what happened. That forty-nine years brings us exactly to the date of the end of the Old Testament and the last prophet, Malachi – 400 BC. So it all fits into God's pattern. During that last section of the Old Testament years, that last forty-nine years, Jerusalem would be rebuilt. You know how under Ezra and Nehemiah it was rebuilt.

Now the next sixty-two "weeks" must elapse before the anointed prince comes to this nation – sixty-two weeks being four hundred and thirty-four years. In Hebrew, the word "anointed" is Messiah – no question who is referred to now. There is some difficulty here with the dating. You can work it out for yourself. It is very interesting to do so. Our calendars are a few years out and Jesus was born in either 4BC or 6BC, so there is a slight discrepancy in our calendars that makes it a little difficult to work out. There are two possibilities of how long a year is to God. One is that it is the Gregorian calendar year that we have of 365 and a quarter days. The other is that it is 360 days – twelve months of thirty days each, which is invariably, through the Bible, the counting of God. You will find it in the book of Revelation that forty-two months is 1260 days – thirty days per month.

I am going to give you a choice of interpretation. First, from the giving of the command to rebuild Jerusalem until the coming of the anointed shall be sixty-nine "weeks"; four hundred and eighty three years. Funnily enough, two systems fit. If the command to rebuild is the command of Artaxerxes to Ezra, in Ezra 7, in 458 BC, then go through four hundred and eighty-three years of 365 and a quarter days and you come to the baptism of Jesus, when the Holy Spirit anointed him.

On the other hand if you take Artaxerxes's command to

Nehemiah in 445 BC (given in Nehemiah chapter two) and take four hundred and eighty-three years of 360 days, you come to the month of Nisan in the year AD29, when Jesus sat on an ass and rode into Jerusalem. Either way, just under five hundred years after the decree to build Jerusalem, the Messiah prince comes to Jerusalem. Isn't God's timing amazing?

So verse twenty-five has come true. Now verse twenty-six does a rather unusual thing. It says, "After the sixty-two weeks" – it doesn't say, "During the seventieth". The Bible is very careful on language; it never wastes a word. After the Messiah comes to Jerusalem, two events will happen. One: the anointed one will be cut off and have nothing. As far as the Jews were concerned, that is exactly what happened. Just a few days after he rode into Jerusalem as their coming prince, they nailed him to a cross. They said, "Away with him. His blood be upon us and our children. Away with him; crucify him." They crucified Jesus, and Daniel said it was going to happen after the sixty-second "week", and it did. He did not have a throne in Israel. A few weeks later, when he ascended to heaven, his disciples were so puzzled they said, "Lord, are you at this time going to restore the kingdom to Israel?" Jesus said, "It's not for you to know the times or dates the Father has set by his own authority." Obviously, it was not yet.

The second thing that was to happen after the sixty-two "weeks" was that the city would again be destroyed. In AD70 the Roman armies came like a flood on that city and they wrecked it and burned the temple to the ground and it has not been built since. These two events occurred in an interval after the sixty-second "week". It says that that interval would go on in wars to the end.

That has been the history of this land and city ever since, and still is. They are still from one war to the next. Jerusalem has known more wars in the few years since the Jews got back into it than it did for many long centuries. Can you see God's plan unfolding before your very eyes? We are living at the end of verse twenty-six. We are right in the wars mentioned there.

So we come to verse twenty-seven, which talks about the last seven years, the last "week". What we are saying is that these whole verses, the prophecy in vv. 24–27, are about the Jews and Jerusalem. They are not about the church; they are not about us Christians or Gentiles, they are about Jerusalem, the Jews: God's nation. When they rejected their anointed prince, God's clock stopped for Israel and it will stop until the seventieth week begins and then start ticking again. As far as Israel is concerned, God's clock has stopped. So the seventy weeks, the four hundred and ninety years, are not yet complete. Now we are used to this. Maybe this week at your work you said you worked forty hours. That doesn't mean you worked non-stop for forty hours. You probably worked for five days of eight hours. Or suppose I asked you, "How long have you lived in your town," and you said, "We moved here ten years ago but we spend six months of the year in France, so I suppose we have been here five years." You see, you can telescope time like this into a total. God's total dealings with Israel: four hundred and ninety years, but during this gap between the sixty-ninth and seventieth, we Gentiles are the heirs to salvation.

When the seventh "week" comes, the last seven years of Israel, what will happen? There is talk of a prince who will do terrible things to them, a ruler who will begin that period by making a treaty with them that they will sign, and they will be fooled. Then, halfway through the seven years, after three and a half years he will turn on them and forbid the Jewish faith to be practised, forbid sacrifice and desolate their holy temple.

Who is this? We have heard of him before. We have been studying him in previous chapters. The book of Revelation in chapters 11, 12 and 13 talks about the three and a half years, the forty-two months, the 1260 days of terrible trouble under the Antichrist. Here we are up against our old enemy, the last world dictator who will wreak his hatred on the Jews, and Jerusalem will suffer more in that three and a half last years than they have ever suffered, but praise God as to what that will do: it is God's way of getting them ready for the final stage of their glorious history, and that is Jesus coming again: Christ to defeat Antichrist.

The Jews will look to him whom they pierced and they will believe. What will be the result? It will be that their iniquity has been atoned for, their sin will end, their transgression will go and righteousness will be established. For the first time, Israel will fulfil her divine vocation. When Israel turns to God, the nations of the world will turn to her and seek her God. The whole dealings of God with Israel will be complete. The four hundred and ninety years will be over. The last seven years of it will be the most terrible, and yet the darkest night before the dawn – and Israel will be saved as a nation.

I can make no other sense of this passage than the picture I have given to you. There are one or two minor problems with my interpretation, but it seems that if we are taking these verses in their simplest, plainest meaning, this is what God is saying and this is what he is going to do for his ancient people.

So we are living in this prophecy. We are living at the end of v. 26 and we are waiting for v. 27 to happen. As Daniel studied scripture to see what happened next, so must we. As Daniel was driven to prayer for his nation, I believe we are too – that we may claim God's Word; claim his glory, and his honour.

10

BY THE TIGRIS
Read Daniel 10

A. SPECIAL CONCERN – 3 weeks (1–4)
    1. When? – time
    2. Why? – manner
B. SPIRITUAL COMFORT – 3 angels (5–19)
    1. Stand
    2. Speak
    3. Listen
C. SUPERNATURAL CONFLICT – 3 princes (20–21)
    1. Persia
    2. Greece

It is very easy to get a wrong impression of Daniel's life from the Bible. It seems to have been an exciting series of sensational happenings that crowded into his life. If he is not interpreting a king's dream then he is watching a king go mad. If he is not reading mysterious writing on a wall, he is being thrown to the lions. It seems that when he went to bed he had marvellous dreams, and when he got up he had visions. He was bumping into angels all over the place, and you look at your own life and you say, "Well, there is just no comparison. Here I am shaving and shopping and washing up and going to the office. How does Daniel's life relate to mine, and why is it that these people in the Bible had such exciting lives with so much evidence of the supernatural, and I struggle on?"

Of course, we are getting a totally wrong impression. The reason is that the Bible only picks out the highlights, the most significant events in Daniel's life. I did some counting and discovered that the book of Daniel only covers five days in the life of Daniel altogether, yet he lived thirty-four thousand days on earth! So what was happening on the other days of Daniel's life? The answer is: he was saying his prayers, getting up, going to the office and running the civil service. Because the book of Daniel has jumped from highlight to highlight to highlight, we think that life in those days was just one exciting series of miracles. You count up the number of miracles in the Bible, realise that the Bible covers fourteen hundred years, and you understand that there were whole generations of the people of God who did not see one miracle. In fact, life consists primarily – for everybody, including Daniel – of very ordinary business, doing what God has told you to do. The special moments stand out because of that ordinary, faithful living for God.

So it is the same with the dreams of Daniel. We forget that so many days of his life were spent being a civil servant. In the same way, we tend to forget that Jesus spent nearly seven thousand days opening a village shop and closing it. I have begun like this to give you some encouragement. As far as we know, Daniel only had four dreams and visions in his life. We come now to the fourth and final one. All four he had in his seventies and eighties. As far as we know, God did not speak to him in this way at other times. So if you are wanting a vision and a dream every week then maybe you are wanting something that even Daniel did not have. So through all those years, until he was sixty-nine years of age, as far as we know, he had no dreams and visions himself. The last one came when he was eighty-six.

This is the one we are going to be looking at from now on. It was the best of the lot, it was the biggest of the lot, it was the most detailed of all four, and it occupies chapters 10–12, bringing us to the end of the book of Daniel. Here we are going to look at the beginning of the vision, the setting in which it came, because just as a dream by night is often related to what has been happening the day before, so a vision in the day is related to what is going on. We shall look at where Daniel was, what he was doing, and why he was doing this, and see how the vision grew out of his ordinary, everyday experience.

We are also going to touch on a very important question: why do we not get immediate answers to prayer sometimes? There is a real answer to that question here, which I hope will help us. Mind you, when the visions did come to Daniel, they were worth waiting for.

I divide this chapter into three headings: *a special concern which was in Daniel's heart* which we read about in verses one to four which led to the vision; *a spiritual comfort that he needed* before he could take the vision (and we will look at the various parts of that spiritual ministry which came from the angels to Daniel); finally we are going to come to the heart of this chapter: *a supernatural conflict that is going on all the time*.

Let us first of all look at the special concern that Daniel has. The details are all important, and the more I study the Bible, the more I am impressed with the fact that God never wastes words. He only tells us that which is necessary to know. Therefore, this preliminary, about when and where it was, is vital. Let us look first at the time. When did this vision come? In the third year of Cyrus: 536 BC. What is so important about that? The answer is that two or three years previously, Babylon, which had taken the people of God in Jerusalem in chains into exile, was finished, and a new empire from the east, Persia (now called Iran) had risen up, overcome Babylon, and therefore a change of government was raising the hopes of God's people that there might be a change of policy and that they might get free.

Sure enough, in the first year of the Persian ruler Cyrus, they were given their freedom. Cyrus made a decree: "You can go home. You can rebuild Jerusalem." That is what happened, and so they began, and the first wave of exiles had gone back. They trekked across the desert – fifty thousand of them, hundreds of miles through the desert, round that Fertile Crescent and back into the land that was theirs. What a moment that must have been when they got there. I remember sitting in a cinema in London watching the film, *Exodus*, and my wife and I were the only Gentiles, I think, in the cinema that night – it was a special night for Israelis to see that marvellous film of how they had gone back to their own land in the twentieth century. The whole audience was so moved. We felt like onlookers – in the film, people were getting off planes and kissing the soil, saying "We've come home. This is where we belong."

The start of the return from Exile in Babylon must have happened just three years before Daniel's vision came. Daniel had not gone. Maybe he was too old for the journey, or maybe, like a good captain on a ship, he was saying, "I'm staying here until I've got them all back home and I'll come with the last lot. My place is here to look after his people and see that those who don't get away straightaway are looked after in the new regime." Or it may be that God wanted him to stay there and die there and never to see his land again. In fact, that is what happened.

That is the background. You might have thought Daniel would have been overjoyed. They are going home! God has opened the door and the exiles were going back rejoicing. You might think they would have celebrated this with great fervour, especially since it was the month of April when they celebrate the Passover. They celebrate the release from Egypt, the end of slavery, the going out, and the coming in to the Promised Land. In the month of April in the year 536 BC you would have thought Daniel would have been feasting, dancing, singing, rejoicing – yet he has been mourning for three whole weeks. He is nibbling at bread; he is drinking water and he won't touch wine, meat, delicacies, fruit. He is just keeping alive and sitting by a river. His face has not been washed. He is miserable, unkempt, unhappy, and he has been like that for three weeks. What has gone wrong?

In fact, poor old Daniel realised that everything was going wrong. Let me tell you four things that had happened in the last previous years. By the way, in these four things you would think I was reading off the present situation of Israel. They are so contemporary. Number one: some Jews had gone back to the Holy Land, but the rest would not go. Fifty thousand had gone and the rest gave them money to go, but would not join them. The situation today is exactly the same; the majority of Jews are still living outside Israel. There are three million of them in New York alone. They will give money, but they are so settled and so assimilated where they are that they are reluctant to go back and it will take some big tragedy to get them to go back.

In Babylon there were millions who should have gone but they had assimilated to the culture and land of Babylon. They had become so settled there after seventy years that they were not willing to uproot themselves and pioneer the land again. They had become merchants, they prospered, and they were settled. That was the first thing that had gone wrong.

The second thing that was going wrong was that those who had gone had started re-building with great enthusiasm, and built an altar to the Lord, laid the foundation of the temple, and then enthusiasm had waned so quickly, as it can do, and the building had slowed and then come to a stop.

The third thing that happened among the fifty thousand Jews who had gone back home to the land is that they were divided, and arguing among themselves. There were renegade Jews who were against the others, and there was trouble within the camp – just as today one of the biggest problems of Israel is that they have so many political parties all trying to get hold of the government.

The fourth thing that was going wrong was that in fact, there were enemies all around the little group of fifty thousand, who were opposing their rebuilding and trying to stop them restoring the land.

All these things were going wrong. Those who had hoped that once they got there everything would be wonderful were now finding that it was not working out. I read the book *O Jerusalem*, an account of the 1948 troubles in the Middle East, and it is tragic to read of returning exiles who had lived for this day all their lives and had come out of ghettos and tremendous suffering and thought, "If I can just at last get there, I'll be alright." They stepped off the planes in 1948, rifles were put in their hands and they were sent to their death within twenty-four hours. This is the atmosphere and it is strangely modern. Can we get back into Daniel's feelings? After seventy years he thought, "Once they get back, everything's going to be fine." Like many another human hope, we have such hopes. We say, "Once we get retired, once we get that little bungalow, everything is going to be lovely." Or, "Once we get that job and do that, everything is going to be fine." Don't you believe it, that is not the way to peace.

God had said it to Daniel again and again, that it is really getting spiritually right with God that will put everything right for you. It is not getting that ideal place to live; it is not getting that little heaven on earth. It is right wherever you are – being right with God. So Daniel is mourning as he realises that this is not a spectacular Exodus.

Back in the days of Egypt, two and a half million people had got out and the Egyptian army had been drowned in the Red Sea, and everything was marvellous. But this time it was not working out like that. It was not spectacular and it was one trouble after another. So Daniel is mourning for three weeks.

Let us look at where he is. He has run away from Babylon, his home. He has travelled thirty-five miles. There are two gigantic rivers nearly two thousand miles long, stretching from what used to be the garden of Eden. The two rivers go down to the Persian Gulf, and at one point they come very near to each other, only thirty-five miles apart, and Babylon is on this river. Daniel has just walked a three-day journey across to the other river. Does he want to get away? He has taken a few men with him, probably Jews. They are going to celebrate the Passover, and he is moving in the opposite direction from Jerusalem, further into the kingdom of Persia. He is sitting by the Tigris river and I wonder if he is imagining this: "This river comes from the Garden of Eden – I wonder if we'll ever get back to Paradise."

The Tigris is more turbulent than the Euphrates. The latter is a wide, sluggish river but the Tigris is swifter, and maybe it reflected Daniel's feelings. Instead of being placid by the Euphrates, he is turbulent and disturbed. But there he sits by the river side, an unkempt, unhappy man, far from home, far from Jerusalem, and even now away from the home he has known for seventy years. The one thing he wants to do is to understand. We are told that he is praying: Lord, I don't understand ... why?

Have you ever felt like this? Lord, I just don't get it. I thought it was all going to be fine and it is not. Do you ever go away by yourself like that and sit and pray and mope? Daniel was doing that. His companions were there with him and nobody talked. If you want to understand a situation, the very best thing you can do is get away, get alone and ask God why.

It took Daniel three weeks to get the answer. We will see why it took three weeks, but he got it. You see, the normal feast of unleavened bread in which you did without those fancy foods was only supposed to last a week. So Daniel could have stopped this after a week and kept within the law of his religion, but he went on three weeks. What is he doing? He is just not going to go back to the good life until the Lord has told him why. He is determined to get an answer. He has sought understanding, so God told him.

It was not very pleasant, as we will see. God was letting Daniel know that his people would have far worse suffering and struggles to go through before the end. They had not seen the worst yet, but one day what he longed for would happen. That is the answer that Daniel got. Now we know the background to the vision. God told Daniel very plainly what it was all about.

The second section in the chapter is the *spiritual comfort* that Daniel needed when the answer came. After sitting for three weeks by that river, something happened. All the men with Daniel got the feeling that there was something supernatural around, something weird going on. Daniel's companions left. People don't like the supernatural; they are afraid when something from another world is coming near, and they have good reason to be afraid. But Daniel stayed.

He remained there because on the other bank of the river he saw someone coming towards him. This person was shining brightly. It looked as if he was dressed in gold from head to foot and even his skin shone. If you and I saw something like this, we would run, I guess, or be petrified, as Daniel was. This figure drew near. It had a face, arms and legs, but this was no human being, this was a visitor from another world. It is strange that we get so interested in science fiction, UFOs and all the rest of it. But the Bible has real experiences whereas other things are just pale reflections and imagined speculation. There can be visitations from the other world, and people have met them, but they have been supernatural beings, God's angels.

The description of this angel is such that many have wondered if it was more than an angel. The description of what he was wearing and how he looked is almost identical to the description in Revelation 1 of our Lord Jesus Christ. Some have therefore said, "Could this be one of the visits that the Son of God paid to earth before he was born in Bethlehem?" The answer is: it could well be. We often forget that Jesus lived long before he was born in Bethlehem – that was just a stage in his existence. He has always been the eternal Son of God. All things were created through him. He was involved in bringing the Hebrews out of Egypt and giving them manna and water in the desert. Jesus was involved all through the Old Testament, though his name was not then "Jesus". The eternal Son of God was there and was taking a hand in Jewish history long before he was born at Bethlehem. So it could be that the person Daniel is meeting now is the very Son of God. I think we must leave the question open, and if you want my own opinion I think it was not – because of some of the things that are said later to Daniel by this person. I think it was a very high angel indeed, coming dressed in his best, if I can put it that way. When the angels had appeared to Daniel up until this point, they had appeared simply as men, in clothes that a human would wear.

But now this could be the same angel that had spoken to Daniel before – that high angel Gabriel, the angel God chooses again and again for special messages to human beings. It was Gabriel who announced to Mary that she was to have a son. This time he is in full regalia.

I would say three things to you about angels. Sometimes, most often, angels help you but are invisible and you are not aware of their presence. It is not childish when you go to bed, to ask God to post an angel at the head of your bed to watch you during the night hours. Most of the stories I know where angels have ministered to people, those concerned have not been aware of their presence. We are encompassed with a great cloud of witnesses but we don't see them. Angels and archangels are joining with us when we praise God.

Secondly, there are occasions when angels actually appear to us but appear in normal human form and dress. Therefore, again, people are not aware that it is an angel. That is why it is literally true that you could have entertained in your house an angel unawares. That is one reason why you should be given to hospitality.

I was reading of a Christian businessman in the US who

was travelling alone in his car and saw a stranger thumbing a lift and he let him in. The stranger hopped into the back of the car and they talked. The hitchhiker lifted the conversation to an extraordinary level – at which the man suddenly felt very near to God. The conversation went on, and the stranger said, "Will you drop me here please?" The driver, so awed was he by the stranger, actually got out and opened the door for him to let him out, then closed the door and got back in. Somebody in a car behind him who knew this businessman said, "What on earth are you doing? You got out of your car on that road, you opened the door, and then you shut it and you got back in and drove on." I tell you that story because the Bible makes it quite clear that you could have seen a person in perfectly normal dress and it could have been one of God's messengers moving through this world. You could have the great privilege one day of meeting an angel in glory who says, "Thanks for that meal, it was good to be with you." Am I getting across the supernatural dimension of life to you?

Missionary after missionary has been protected in the field. Sometimes, as with one well-known missionary whose books you may have read, they prayed for protection in a lonely place because they were sleeping in a hut at night, and there were enemies who came to attack but they did not do so, because they saw "soldiers" standing to attention all around the hut. The missionary never saw them and never knew they were there. The hosts of the Lord encamp around those who fear him.

One of the good things about Christmas is that it is the one time in the year that people begin to think about angels. I am afraid we treat them as tinsel and we dress them up with wings and harps and the rest of it, and stick them up in the shop windows. They don't often appear like that on earth. If they did, we would certainly not entertain them unawares!

BY THE TIGRIS *Daniel 10*

But they do appear as human beings. Sometimes an angel can appear in glory – in heavenly, not earthly, dress. They can come in shining brightness, and this is what happened here.

So believe me, when they come like that you would have had the same reaction as Daniel did – his knees turned to water. After all, he was an elderly man, but he collapsed and fell on the ground and was in no fit state to converse with this messenger of God. It was then that the ministry of spiritual comfort came from three separate angels. It is lovely how God sends a group of angels to help. After all, Jesus once said to his disciples, "Don't you realise I've got ten thousand angels just waiting for my orders." Daniel had three here. The first was the one who had already spoken, and he began the spiritual comfort ministry – to "comfort" means to strengthen, and he touched Daniel, lifted him up off the ground. "Don't be frightened, come on stand up." In a lovely way, the old man Daniel, on his hands and knees, pulled himself up and stood there, but he was still trembling. Then, when this angel spoke to him, Daniel was struck dumb. It says he ran out of breath. Have you ever done that? You get up in front of a crowd and start speaking. You soon find what it is to run out of breath. Daniel felt like that. He just got sheer nerves and couldn't talk. He said, "I can't talk to you." Another angel came and touched his lips. You know, if you are going to speak to heaven you may need a heavenly touch to do so.

The third ministry that came to him was when a third angel came and said, "Do not be afraid, O man highly esteemed." That love takes the fear away and Daniel then feels stronger. Here are three steps of lifting a person into the presence of God. It takes supernatural ministry to make me stand before God, to make me speak to God, and above all to make me strong enough to listen and eager to hear what he is going to say and not be afraid.

Isn't that a lovely little picture of spiritual comfort? So here is Daniel standing, and he says, "Speak, my lord, since you have given me strength." God loves Daniel and is not going to hurt him. Now Daniel is wide open to receive the vision. In fact, if God is going to speak to us in supernatural ways he needs to minister to us at these three levels or we will be so scared stiff we will run away.

This may be the most startling and perhaps the most important feature of this chapter: here is the revelation that there are bad angels as well as good ones, and there is warfare between them, and they are struggling with each other. Some angels are trying to help us and some angels are trying to hinder us. I want you to get this very firmly in your mind: the real warfare that is going on in our world is not with flesh and blood but principalities and powers; world rulers of darkness and spiritual hosts of wickedness in heavenly places.

Let us go back to v. 13 and ask why was it that Daniel had to pray for three weeks before he got an answer to his prayers. Have you had this experience – when you have prayed and prayed and the heavens seem like brass, and it doesn't seem to be getting through, and you make the awful mistake of thinking that God is not listening? Let me tell you this, that when Daniel prayed for twenty-one days God heard him on the very first day, but the answer didn't get through until the twenty-first day. Daniel made the mistake we all make: thinking that if the answer is delayed, God has not heard.

But the angel is saying to Daniel: on the very first day that you fasted and prayed, at the beginning of your asking for understanding, at the beginning of your search, God heard and he set things in motion in answer to your prayer. So whether you feel that God is listening or not, whether you feel that he heard that prayer or not, cling to this: that before you call, he hears and answers. He hears when any child of his cries. You don't need to worry about that – his ear is open.

Well then, why didn't the answer come? The answer is that an angel was dispatched immediately with the answer. One of God's messengers was sent straight away, but he could not get through. Why not? Because another angel, an evil one, stopped him for three weeks. Now are you getting the sense of supernatural conflict? There are good angels in our world seeking to help God's people and to fulfil God's purposes, but they can be delayed or stopped. There is a struggle going on, and there are evil spirits in our world that can stop answers to prayer. The battle goes on, and for those three weeks the angels were locked in conflict and the angel of God couldn't get through to Daniel.

It is interesting that the devil is often called "the prince of the power of the air". The air was, as it were, the belt. The atmosphere is a kind of layer between us and God and the heavens. So the angel left the highest heaven but could not get through to Daniel because the prince of the power of the air and the spirit of that prince blocked him. Two angels are equally matched in strength and they struggled and they couldn't get through. Nothing happened until another angel joined in the fight. "Michael came," says this angel. "He helped me, and the two of us broke through, and three weeks after you prayed we got through to you with the answer."

Furthermore, there is something even more devastating here, and I want you to grasp this answer: do you notice that this evil angel was called the Prince of Persia? That is not referring to the emperor, Cyrus. Here we have the extraordinary truth that there are evil angels who are princes of nations. It is a biblical insight that explains your daily newspaper. In other words, here we have a prince of Persia and the angel says it is going to be a prince of Greece (who would come next) and we are going to have to fight against these princes.

Do you know what Jesus called the devil? He said that the devil is the prince of this world. But the prince of this world appoints evil angels as princes of nations. He says, "You be prince of Asia", or: "Control Persia and keep that country away from God"; and, "You be prince of Greece." I am going to develop this further. In all our present troubles in the world, again and again, people get a sense that someone is behind all this. Isn't that true? They make the mistake of assuming it is a human being. So they are looking under the beds for plots, and everybody is trying to find out who is behind it. They offer all sorts of erratic speculations as to who is responsible. They are right in sensing that someone is behind it all. They are wrong in saying it is flesh and blood. Most people are not aware of spiritual forces. They think it must be a human group and they try to identify it. Think of the history of Germany in the 1930s. How could an upstart little corporal have led a nation into such horrors? Who is behind it? I tell you, there was a prince of Germany.

I have looked at other countries and have seen that leaders are sometimes like helpless pawns being pushed around, and I say, "Who is behind all this?" I look at Britain, and I say, "Who is behind all these troubles? Who is building up problems until we are going to be in real trouble?" I tell you, Satan has appointed a prince of this country. Now when you get this insight and you read your daily newspaper, you say that we are wrestling not against flesh and blood but against principalities and powers and spiritual hosts of wickedness in the heavenlies and world rulers of darkness. That is the biblical diagnosis of trouble. That is what is happening to our world. When we realise that, we then realise why praying for our world is such a struggle – because if you pray for our world you are putting yourself on the front line. You will need the whole armour of God. It is going to be a mighty struggle to pray for our world because it is a spiritual, supernatural conflict. But praise be to God, there are not just evil princes, there are good ones.

This chapter ends with a mention of Michael, Prince of Israel. The theme will go on into chapters eleven and twelve, right to the end of history when there is a resurrection and a judgment and God's people are set free. Michael will be key in this. So there are good angels as well. Who is going to win: the good angels or the bad ones? There is this spiritual warfare; I guess that you might think that I have gone crazy now, but I am trying to tell you the sober truth about what is wrong with our world. We see symptoms, but the real warfare is ongoing. Who is going to win?

The angel has come to tell Daniel about the future: what is already written in "the Book of Truth" (see v. 21). The Bible was still being written – Daniel would write another bit of scripture in his diary that night. God has already written his book. History is "his story" and it is already complete. God has written the whole of history in "the Book of Truth". The angel came and explained that he came to tell of something already written in that book, in God's writing.

In God's book in which everything is written, it is not the prince of Persia or the prince of Greece who enables Alexander to overrun a world with ruthless ambition. It is not the prince of America, nor the prince of Germany, nor the prince of Britain who wins. Michael, the Prince of Israel, and the angels of God will win.

When that warfare is over, this earth will have peace and prosperity. All troubles we have been living with will be a thing of the past, like a nightmare when you have woken up. Daniel is now ready to listen.

11

NORTH AND SOUTH
Read Daniel 11:1–35

A. GOD OF HISTORY (1–2)
    1. Persia (1–2)
       a. Present ruler (Darius under Cyrus)
       b. Successors (Cambyses, Smerdis, Darius I)
       c. Attacking Greece (Xerxes I)
    2. Greece (3–4)
       a. Bad emperor (Alexander the Great)
       b. Four generals (Lysimachus, Cassander, Ptolemy, Seleucus)
    3. Egypt and Syria (5–30)
       a. Rivalry
            i. South (Ptolemy line)
            ii. North (Seleucus/Antiochus line)
       b. Revenge – Egypt on top
            i. Idolatry (Ptolemy Euergetes)
            ii. Ignominy (Seleucus Callinicus)
       c. Repression – Syria on top
            i. Territory (Antiochus the Great)
            ii. Taxation (Seleucus Philopater)
            iii. Tyranny (Antiochus Epiphanes)
    4. Israel (31–35)
       a. Persecution (Antiochus Epiphanes)
       b. Purification (Judas Maccabeus)
B. GOD OF HUMANITY
    1. Divine providence
       a. He knows the future
       b. He plans the future
       c. He reveals the future
    2. Human purpose
       a. Stand firm
       b. Do exploits
       c. Bring understanding
       d. Endure suffering
       e. Be refined
       f. Find rest

We are in the book of Daniel so we are concentrating on predictions, and we have reached a chapter which is unique among all the predictions of the Bible. God is so wise that he knows how much of the future we can cope with, how much to tell us, and how much to keep hidden. I thank him that he has hidden much of the future from us. Otherwise I don't think we could stand it. But what he has revealed is important and is just what we need to know. So Daniel 11 must be necessary to us as Christians or it would not be in the Bible. But when I read it to a congregation I sometimes see an expression on some faces as if to say, "What on earth has that to do with us today?" We might be surprised.

Let me remind you that prophecy is a miracle. The Bible itself is a miracle. Man has no capacity for foretelling the future in detail, we always write up history after it has happened. Only God has the power to write history before it happens. Therefore there are those who believe that it is impossible for it to happen. If you don't believe in God, and if you don't believe in a God of miracles, then you think it impossible to forecast the future in such detail as this. So many scholars have tried to claim that Daniel 11 must be a forgery written up after the events it describes and then given the name "Daniel" to get it into the Bible, and that what we read here is a fraud and a lie, and that it was not an angel foretelling the future but somebody writing up the past.

The first person to say this was a man called Porphyry who lived some sixteen hundred years ago. He was a Phoenician living in Sicily, who spent months at the age of forty writing fifteen volumes attacking Christianity – amazing industry for such a sceptic. Volume 12 contains an attack on the book of Daniel. His argument runs like this: that Daniel 11

197

can't be true because it is too accurate. It is such a laughable argument. He then goes through the chapter, showing that every single detail came true and thereby "proving" to people that it could not possibly be written by Daniel. It is indeed laughable when you believe in a God who knows the future, but that is the kind of logic that the unbeliever gets himself into. To Porphyry it seemed that he was arguing perfectly logically, and to him the accuracy of this chapter gave the lie to the Word of God. To us, the accuracy of this chapter does precisely the opposite. It proves that God is true; let every man be a liar including Porphyry. Now I am never worried by attacks on the Christian faith. I am never worried by attacks on the Bible. God causes even the wrath of man to praise him.

When Porphyry wrote those fifteen volumes, and particularly volume 12 on Daniel, it stimulated a saintly scholar in Bethlehem called Jerome to write a commentary on the book of Daniel and to do something he had always felt like doing but now knew to be necessary. That commentary would be the finest thing written about this book for a thousand years. So out of that attack came a book that helped, and still helps, for I have a copy. It still helps people today to understand the Bible. The argument of Porphyry is a boomerang, and the accuracy of this chapter points to the truth of God's Word.

Granted that God can know and foretell the future, how could man get hold of it from God? How could a man called Daniel write down things that were yet to happen in the future? Daniel 11:1–35 covers a period of 365 years. Daniel says he wrote down that history of one year for every day in the year, or every day in a leap year; he wrote it down six years before it opens, so that he was writing all this six years before the first thing came to pass. Then it started, and for the next three hundred and sixty-six years it happened.

In these 35 verses there are 135 predictions of the future – an average of four details per verse about things that are going to happen. Do you know that every single one of those 135 things came true to the letter? I am afraid I am going to give you a history lesson. (That is a subject I hated at school and I dropped it as soon as I could!) How did Daniel get hold of this? He is an elderly man, sitting by a river, unhappy, unkempt, fasting and praying for three weeks. What was the matter? Daniel says he doesn't understand what on earth is happening and what things are coming to. He was trying to get an answer from God about what was happening.

Daniel feels like many of us feel. You look at the world, you read your newspaper, you watch the television news, and you say, "What on earth is happening? What are things coming to?" You think the world is out of control. What is God doing, and where is he? As we noticed in the last chapter, Daniel was determined to get an answer from God, and we know now that the first day he prayed, God heard and sent him an angel to give him an answer. There had been a battle in the supernatural places between the good angel carrying the answer to Daniel and the bad angel who was trying to keep Persia from God. The good angel and the bad angel struggled for three weeks, because the bad angels and the devil do not want the world to hear what is going to happen. That is why the devil keeps people from the book of Daniel and the book of Revelation. The devil wants us to be disturbed and frightened. He wants us to despair, he wants us to feel things are out of control, so when the revelation of the future is coming, then one of the devil's angels tries to stop it. But another angel came to the rescue of the good one, the two good ones dealt with the bad one, and the good one got through. Three weeks after Daniel started praying, that angel came to tell him the future.

Now 11:1–35 divides into four periods. In the first, Persia

is the main nation involved; in the second section, Greece takes the stage; in the third section, interestingly enough, Egypt and Syria come to the fore. By a strange irony they are in the centre of the stage of world history right now. That is not a coincidence. The fourth section is concerned with Israel, caught between Egypt and Syria. Martin Luther said that Israel was caught between the door and the hinges of Egypt and Syria. When they closed onto each other it was Israel that got trapped. Somebody else has said, "If you live in the middle of a crossroads, you're liable to get run over" – and that is what has happened to Israel again and again.

Let us run through the history that has fulfilled the prophecy. I will mention the verse that I am in, and then state what history did, and you see if you can tie it up. Bear in mind that various translations of the Bible do put some phrases differently, and there is still a little uncertainty about the meaning of some of the phrases.

First of all then, in v. 1 we have Persia. In vv. 1–2, Persia has now taken over from Babylon. Daniel had lived in Babylon most of his life, and then, as we have seen, on that infamous night of Belshazzar's feast, Babylon had fallen and Persia was now the centre of the world stage. Cyrus was its emperor and he appointed Darius to look after the former province of Babylon. So, in a sense, Daniel is under Cyrus, but more directly under Darius. The angel telling Daniel the future says, "It was I who enabled Darius to do what was right in his first year." Darius did two things that were right in his first year. One was he let Daniel out of the lions' den after an angel had shut the lions' mouths, and secondly, Darius had also passed on the decree of Cyrus the emperor that the Jews could go home. The angel is saying, "Why do you think these two things happened in Darius's first year? I was around and now I am going to take the story from there and tell you how it is going to develop."

After Cyrus, after this emperor, after Darius, there will be three more kings and indeed there were. Then says the angel, "There will be a fourth king of Persia who will become very rich and use that wealth to attack Greece." The man who fulfilled this to the letter was Xerxes I. He became very rich, built up a huge army and said, "I want Greece." He made the biggest mistake of his life in going to invade Greece because the Greeks never forgave him. The grudge they held led to a young man called Alexander (who became Alexander the Great) saying, "If ever I get the chance I will take Persia to be my own for invading my country of Greece." So Xerxes was the invader of Greece but he was disastrously defeated in 480 BC.

In vv. 3–4, the scene switches to Greece. We have already looked at Alexander the Great, who avenged Greece by defeating Persia. He is, of course, the he-goat of Daniel 8.

Now v. 4 says something rather surprising: "His sons will not inherit his kingdom." He married two wives and had a son by each of them. Both the wives were Persian. He married them both in an act of personal revenge, as it were, to bring Persia under his control. One of those sons was murdered before Alexander died, and the other was born just after he died and was murdered soon afterwards so there were no sons of Alexander left to inherit. Bear in mind that we are reading history in the Bible, written beforehand, not afterwards.

Finally, the empire was divided up between four generals. One took the north, one the east, one the west, and one the south. Literally, it was divided up into four smaller bits ruled over by the four generals of Alexander: Lysimachus, Cassander, Ptolemy, and Seleucus. From now on there are only two parts of the world that concern us here. Firstly, there is the area we call Syria today. They didn't call it Syria in those days, so the name doesn't appear in this chapter, again proving the accuracy that this has as a prediction. If this had been written after the event, the name "Syria" would have appeared because then it was known. The two areas that concern us are Syria in the north, now referred to as the north, where the line of Seleucus reigned; and Egypt in the south where the line of Ptolemy reigned. These were the door and the hinge, and in between was Israel. So you can see that the centre of history is Israel, and what is north of Israel is referred to as "the north". I would say that Israel is the hinge, Egypt is the door, and Syria is the doorpost. World history hinged on Israel and it still does so.

Let us look from now on at vv. 5–35. Our concern is with Egypt and Syria. This passage covers only 162 years. In v. 5 the first two kings were Ptolemy Soter (or Ptolemy saviour) in the south (Egypt) and Seleucus Nicator in the north. Both of them, after governing those two areas as generals, took the title "king" at the same moment. This began the rivalry between the two. They both wanted to be king not just governor general, and so they became rivals. In v. 6, the next Ptolemy in Egypt called himself Philadelphus (brotherly love). He wanted to govern Syria as well, so he persuaded Antiochus in the north to divorce his wife Laodice and marry his own daughter. The union did not work out either as a marriage or as an attempt to unite the two royal families. When Ptolemy died, Antiochus felt free to take his wife Laodice back, but Laodice wasn't having this. She was not going to be pushed out and taken back. She murdered Antiochus and his son, and that particular family came to an end.

In vv. 7–9, there is now a seesaw battle between Syria in the north and Egypt in the south. The brother of Baronies in the south, another Ptolemy called Euergetes (Benefactor), attacked the king of the north who is now Seleucus Callinicus and he kills Laodice now for murdering his sister. What a story, isn't it! Now he is victorious throughout the northern kingdom. So now they are not rivals – Egypt is on top of Syria. That is not going to last for long because in v. 8, when Ptolemy comes back from defeating Syria, he brings back some idols with him that had been taken from Egypt nearly three hundred years previously. When he brought them back to the people of Egypt, they welcomed him with this cry, "Benefactor, Benefactor." So he got the name Euergetes from then on. In v. 9, the Syrian comes back to the attack, loses his fleet in a storm, is defeated, and dies after a fall from his horse.

Now we move to vv. 10–19. Let us recall the picture. In vv. 5–6 Egypt and Syria are rivals; in vv. 7–9, Egypt gets the upper hand. In vv. 10ff., Syria gets the upper hand, and let us see how they did it. Two brothers began it: Seleucus and Antiochus, but Seleucus was assassinated by mutinous troops in a battle in Asia Minor. This left Antiochus III, who took the title "the Great" and was determined to be the greatest. He came to power at the age of eighteen and spent his life fighting to avenge his father's humiliation. Finally, he achieved the extension of territory as far south as Gaza, which was the outer line of Egypt's defence. In v. 11, Ptolemy V (*Philopater*, which means love of father) met Alexander the Great with an army of 7,000 soldiers, 5,000 cavalry and seventy-three "tanks", only the tanks of those days were elephants. In 217 BC, at a place called Rapier, Antiochus the Great was totally defeated – 10,000 of his soldiers were dead and 4,000 taken prisoner. He himself only just escaped.

In v. 12, Ptolemy, an indolent and indulgent king who thought that was all he needed to do, went back to Egypt and feasted, and he failed to follow through.

Antiochus the Great decided to go east. He went as far east as India, and built up his strength, captured troops and money from his eastern campaign, and came back and was ready for a second go at Egypt. In fact, in v. 13, when Ptolemy and his queen had died, Antiochus attacked Egypt and defeated their army at a little place called Panias, at the headwaters of the Jordan at the foot of Mount Hermon.

The Egyptian general Scopus fled to Sidon, a fortified city of Egypt on the coast. So in v. 15, we find a little later that Sidon is besieged and taken, in spite of an unsuccessful attempt by three Egyptian generals to break the siege. But v. 14 tells us that some renegade Jews sided with Antiochus the Great to get rid of the Egyptians. They could not have made a bigger mistake because they were going to introduce Syrian occupation. In v. 16, Antiochus makes the mistake of occupying Israel as a military base. He laid waste the country to support his troops. In v. 17, a new power is rising on the horizon – Rome. Antiochus now sought to unite with Egypt against Rome. He had a very beautiful teenage daughter called Cleopatra. He gave his daughter Cleopatra to the king of Egypt who was only seven years old at the time (the marriage was not consummated for another five years). His hope was that she would work secretly over this boy king and bring Egypt under his control. The snag was that she was not having any and she always took the side of the boy against her dad. The whole thing came to nothing.

In v. 18, Antiochus the Great scorned Roman power. He said, "Asia does not concern them, the Romans, and I am not subject to their orders." He refused their ambassadors, decided to conquer Greece himself instead of letting the Romans take it, and was humiliatingly defeated by the Roman consul Scipio at the battle of Thermopylae, and then at Magnesia.

In v. 19, such were the harsh conditions of peace with Rome that Antiochus came home a broken man and was killed while trying to plunder a temple. He had opened Asia for Rome. In v. 20, his son (who must have loved his father because he called himself *Philopater,* "love father", Seleucus IV) found he needed an awful lot of money to keep Rome happy, to keep peace and quiet.

The Romans said, "We'll keep peace for you if you give us protection money." We have heard of that elsewhere. So poor Seleucus had to find a lot of money and he decided to raise taxes from Israel and to take the treasures of the temple. So he became known as the tax collector king. When he got to the temple in Jerusalem he was about to plunder it of its treasure. He sent his finance minister Heliodoris to collect all this and he saw an apparition, then went home and poisoned Seleucus.

So now we come to vv. 21–35. We come to the final king, of whom we have heard before. He was the most terrible one – Antiochus Epiphanes (*Epiphanes* means glorious), the little horn of Daniel 7. Syria's power was now declining. Rome was overshadowing the Middle East, and Rome would be the power on the world stage when Jesus was born.

Antiochus Epiphanes was frustrated and so he turned his bitter frustration into persecution of God's people, and no tyrant was worse than this man who desecrated her temple, tried to wipe out her religion and impose Greek culture. In v. 21 he is called a vile man or corrupt man. What did it mean? Well, he associated with prostitutes and actresses, engaged even in public copulation as a defiance of decency. He was known for his avaricious indulgence, for his cunning and intrigue. The direct heir to the Syrian throne was a young man called Demetrius, but he was already held as a hostage in Rome. The other next in line was the baby of Seleucus IV, a child called Antiochus as well. Antiochus Epiphanes posed as the baby's guardian, flattered the nation, and by bribing them with offers of easier taxation came to power in Syria.

In v. 22, at first, his military activity was very successful.

He gained peace with Rome by paying the arrears of tax with bribes, then he invaded Egypt and defeated them between Gaza and the Nile Delta. But on the way south to defeat Egypt, he called in at Jerusalem and murdered Onnias, the high priest, the prince of the covenant, the leader of Israel at the time.

In v. 23, though he didn't have many helpers and his was not a large nation, he was now able to control Egypt using two of his nephews.

In v. 34, he did something that no one had done before. He scattered wealth. The fact is that Antiochus Epiphanes loved to rob rich areas like Galilee and then he would walk down the streets throwing coins, and of course, as you can imagine, you can soon get popularity that way. So he would redistribute wealth. Hitherto, when rulers got wealth they kept it for themselves or spent it on the army. He was a prodigal in more ways than one.

In v. 25, he makes another expedition to Egypt, hoping to capture Alexandria. He had chariots, cavalry and elephants. He managed to corrupt Egypt's court so that the Egyptian king's own leaders turned against him. There was a military coup in Egypt in which the king lost his throne. In v. 26, this led to Egypt's defeat. In v. 27, Antiochus and the Egyptian king sat at a table pretending to each other, trying to base treaties on lies, each trying to outwit the other. Both failed because God's time had not yet come. We will come back to that.

In v. 28, when Antiochus the Great returned north, he went back to Israel and he coveted the wealth of the temple. He massacred forty thousand Jews, sold the same number into slavery, and Jason the high priest fled across the Jordan to Amon. In v. 29, he made another expedition to Egypt, capturing his own nephew Ptolemy Philometor, but was forced to retreat because he could not capture Alexandria.

In v. 30, we find that Egypt sent an embassy to Rome. Remember Cleopatra is still around. Rome sent ships from Cyprus, and the Roman consul Lenas demanded Antiochus withdraw from Egypt. Antiochus had to leave in a very bad mood, realising this was the end of his ambitions.

In vv. 31–35, Antiochus, angry, resentful, a failure, knowing his days are numbered by Rome, turns to the little nation of Israel. Have you noticed that a bully, when defeated by someone bigger than himself, turns on a little chap? The whole of Antiochus's wrath came against Israel.

We come now to the most important part of the chapter. The Jews became his scapegoat. You can read all about his savage persecution in the Apocryphal books 1 and 2 Maccabees if you are interested. He uses sympathisers within Israel – he had quislings already there. He had renegade Jews already with him, and using them he closed the temple for worship. He forbade sacrifice to Yahweh. Then he erected in the temple a statue of Jupiter, the god of war. Then, as we noted earlier, he did something horrible. He took a pig, the unclean animal to the Jew, and he sacrificed that pig on the altar of the temple in Jerusalem. The smell of roast pork filled the city. Nothing could be imagined that would insult or offend Jewish religious sensibilities like that. Antiochus Epiphanes goes down in history as the one who erected the abomination of desolation in the place where it ought not to be. In Matthew 24:15, talking about the end of the world, Jesus taught that when you see that happen again, when you see the abomination of desolation where it ought not to be, then you take note, the end is very near.

In Daniel 11:32, this precipitated the revolt of the Maccabees family under its father, the priest Matthias. Maccabees means "hammerer" – a significant nickname. Under the leadership of one of the seven sons, Judas Maccabees, Antiochus's troops were turned out of Israel, and for a few years Israel had her independence and her own king before Rome came to occupy the land.

In vv. 33–35, there is a description of the surprising effects of this persecution on the people of Israel, and I will be dealing with them in a little more detail.

This chapter tells me three things about God. First of all, God knows the future – nothing could be clearer. With 135 details all coming true, you have to bow down and say, "O God, you know what's going to happen next week, next year, next century." God knows the future even though we don't. He can see into the distant future. He has this power to the *n*th degree – but is that all? Is this prophecy the result of God knowing the future? No, there is something more. The second thing this chapter tells me is that God *plans* the future. It is not the kind of knowledge that God knows what men are going to do. It is the kind of knowledge that is based on the fact that God knows what *he* is going to do. In other words, these things happen because God plans them, not just because he knows people are going to behave this way. We are right into predestination, and the Bible teaches predestination, make no mistake about that. God decides what is going to happen. People get so worked up about the doctrine of predestination, especially unbelievers. Christians have their questions and problems, but unbelievers hate this. People come to me and say, "Well, what about freewill?" and I say, "Well, what about God's free will? Did you ever think about that?" The way some human beings talk about their freewill, you would think that God had to do what they wanted! But I say that God alone has the greatest freewill and he exercises it.

People say, "How do you line up predestination and freewill?" Simple: predestination is *God's* freewill. That is how you get the two together; that is where you start. This chapter tells me that God actually plans for things to happen; he makes them happen. It is God's hand that is on the steering wheel of history, and that comes out in two ways in the chapter. One is in the phrase "at the appointed time" which occurs three times in the passage we are studying. Who appoints the times? Man doesn't. At the appointed time, prophecy is always fulfilled on schedule – and it is God's schedule, not ours. The other thing is that this chapter says (did you notice?) that certain things did not happen that man tried to do because God had not appointed the time yet. In other words, this is a chapter of predestination. The unbeliever loathes that doctrine for the simple reason that it hurts our pride, it robs us of our power, and it threatens our freedom. We like to think that man is the captain of his fate and the master of his soul. We like to think that we are in charge of history, that we can get together and decide what is going to happen. Let me tell you from this chapter: when politicians get around a conference table, if God has not appointed peace at that time for them, there is nothing they can do to get it. If God has appointed peace, then they will find it.

Doesn't that affect your feelings about what is happening as reported in news media? When you become a believer and when you submit your freewill to God's freewill, you discover in your experience a freedom you never had before, and more than that, predestination becomes for you a most precious truth. No longer need you be afraid that history is out of control; no longer need you be afraid that it is in the hands of politicians. It is not in their hands, it is in the hands of Almighty God. When you are in line with *his* freewill, what a comfort that is.

Predestination becomes a precious truth, for the word means to decide destiny beforehand. God has decided the destiny of our world. He has decided the destiny of nations. He decided when the British Empire would come to an end, and it came to an end when he planned it. He decides when nations rise and fall. He allots their boundaries in time and space. Paul said that at Athens.

So, finally – God knows the future. He plans the future, and he tells the future. Why should God tell us what is going to happen? Certainly not to satisfy intellectual curiosity. People want to know, they are intellectually curious, but God's purpose is practical and moral. Why does he want to tell us? I think we can find the answer in the last few verses of the passage: by telling us, God is helping us to meet the future; his aim is to strengthen his people.

If you want a text for this study, here it is: those who know God shall be strong and do exploits. People say, "Well, predestination, if it is all settled and fixed then we will just sit back and wait for it to happen." Don't you believe it! If you really grasp predestination you will get up and go. You really get on with the job. You do great things. But let us go through six things that are mentioned here one after the other, which happen to God's people when they know the future. Number one, God's people will stand firm. When the world is shattered, when people around us say, "What on earth are things coming to?" – you say: "I'll tell you what they're coming to if you want to know..." when the whole wide earth is shaking, then Christians will stand firm. That is going to be one of the things that will more and more differentiate Christians from others in these last days. As the world shakes, Christians will get firmer and say, "We're getting nearer; we know how it is going to turn out; we know what's going to happen." Stand firm!

Secondly, we will do exploits – for when we are in line with God's pattern, he graciously allows us to be his co-workers, and we want to get up and on with it. We want to hasten the day of his coming if we can. It leads us not to be passive and do nothing but to be active and get on with the job. So God's people, who know God – not just who know the Bible or who know the future, but those who know God – will stand firm and do heroic things.

Do you know that Judas Maccabees read this chapter and it inspired him to lead the revolt against Antiochus Epiphanes because he knew that the days of Antiochus were numbered? The Bible had said so. So with great confidence he got on with the job.

Thirdly, God's people will bring understanding. There will be a great ministry of teaching when these disturbances come. Those with understanding will teach many others and spread the news. You have a ministry of teaching to your neighbours – to help them understand what is happening. When disturbing days come, you can teach them what is happening, who is in charge, why it is happening, where it is going to lead. You ought to be able to comment with people on the train who are reading a paper, and help them to understand what they read, even before you help them to understand the Bible.

Fourthly, God's people will endure suffering. When God tells us the future he is honest and he says it will be dangerous. Some may be killed, some burned by fire. That happened in the times of Antiochus Epiphanes and I tell you it is going to happen at the end of history. God's people are going to suffer, and great troubles are coming.

But, fifthly, they will be refined. Suffering always does God's people good. Maybe that is why we are such weak Christians in this country – we don't suffer as much as elsewhere. But don't worry if suffering comes. We are told that "it smelts and it sifts." Those are the two verbs here: *smelting* the dross away; *sifting* the true from the false. You might find that your congregation would halve if suffering comes to your town, but I tell you what, you would have a stronger church. God's people will be purged and purified.

Suffering helps God's people. It strengthens them. It purifies them. It gets them ready for the future.

Finally, God's people will find rest. God has already marked his calendar with the date when all the sufferings of his people will come to an end and all trials will be over.

So God's people will find rest, but I affirm this solemnly in the name of the Lord: when God's people find rest and know that from then on there will be no more trouble, no more trial, no more suffering, that is when the sufferings of all the others will begin. God's people, alone in the universe, are those who can look forward to an end to trouble. Isn't God merciful – that he should show us enough of the future to be strong, to do great things, to teach others the way to suffer, and to know that one day trouble will be over?

I put it this way: when conditions in the world get worse, the condition of God's people gets better. When things go down, we look up, for the day of our redemption draws nigh. The angel had come to let Daniel know what would happen in the future. Daniel's prayers had been heard.

12

THE VERY END
Read Daniel 11:36–12:13

A. ISRAEL'S PRIVATIONS (11:36–12:3)
    1. Deification of Antichrist (36–39)
    2. Destruction of Israel (40–45)
    3. Deliverance of Michael (1–3)
       a. Ruin
       b. Redemption
       c. Resurrection
       d. Reward

B. DANIEL'S PREDICTIONS (4–13)
    1. Deferment of publication (4)
    2. Duration of persecution (5–8a)
    3. Date of peace (8b–13)

In chapter 11 we have the main content of the vision of the future, and now the vision continues. I broke it at the end of v. 35 for a particular reason: as you move on to the end of chapter 11, to the rest of the vision, there are equally detailed predictions about Israel and the nation to the north of her (which we now call Syria) and the nation to the south of her (which is still called Egypt), yet none (or very few) of the predictions beyond v. 36 have in fact been fulfilled yet.

There is no known historical event that corresponds, for example, to the last five verses of this chapter. This is puzzling. The Bible is never wrong, so why did these events not happen when the first thirty-five verses were fulfilled to the letter, right up to the time of the terrible persecution of Israel by Antiochus Epiphanes? One of the clues lies in the phrase at the beginning of v. 40 – "at the time of the end". In fact, the little word "end" occurs about a dozen or more times between now and the end of this vision – the end of the prophecy of Daniel.

The simple reason is that it is still future to us. Just as the first thirty-five verses of chapter 11 have all been fulfilled to the letter, so everything at the end of chapter eleven will most certainly come true. You may live to see these details being worked out, and you may read about these things in your daily newspaper – events in the Middle East. We can expect history to repeat itself and Israel once again to be caught between Syria and Egypt. We can expect this Middle East situation to be a feature of the last days. People have asked, "What grounds have you for saying this?" Well, this is my ground: the same countries are involved in a different period at the end of history. Now having said that, I am afraid it is not as easy as to say that up to v. 35 is past – over two thousand years ago – and v. 36 onwards is future. I can say that v. 40 onwards is future, but vv. 36–39 are a puzzle.

Some of the content of these verses does apply to Antiochus Epiphanes. Some of the things here described of the king are true of him, but some are not.

The only explanation I can come to, and it seems to me a valid one, is that vv. 36–39 are sliding or overlapping between past and future, sliding from one king to another, almost unnoticed – telescoping over two thousand years of history into one account. What makes me say that? Why does the Bible not abruptly finish the predictions that have passed and start the predictions of the future? Why is there an overlap between, so that the history that is past goes right on to v. 39 but the history that is future starts at v. 36 and you have four verses overlapping?

I have hinted at the reason before. Antiochus Epiphanes was the worst and the last tyrant of the Old Testament period. He was quite the worst persecutor of the Jews. In the things he did and said, in the very length of time that he oppressed Israel, you have a prefiguring, pattern, type and forecast of the last and worst tyrant of the New Testament period, whom we call "Antichrist" because we do not yet know his name. Antichrist will be someone claiming to be the prince and saviour of the whole human race. Now it is the astonishing likeness of these two which explains the overlap. As you look at Antiochus you see a picture of Antichrist. It is as if you are looking at two people through a telescope, and you see them both together, and they are so much the same that you think you have seen one person with a kind of double image, and this is the kind of thing that is happening in vv. 36–37.

So let me treat these as having a double fulfilment. You have here a description of a king who thinks he is God. Antiochus Epiphanes thought that. I had never been interested really in historical relics, but since I got to know what the Bible said about history and the future I have found myself interested. One of the most fascinating things you can do is to go around the British Museum with a Bible in your hand. I have got a handbook that tells you everything in the British Museum that is from the Bible. It is fascinating to go around and read your Bible and look into the glass cases. Now if you look at the coins of Antiochus Epiphanes, you can see on them his growing obsession with himself as "god". You can see the change of titles. First of all, *Epiphanes* – glorious, then he changed the title and called himself the "manifest" or the "incarnate one"; and finally, on the last coins he minted, he puts the word *theos* which means "God". It is the same word as our "theology" – study of God. The first step towards this man's growing obsession with himself as a deity was when he disregarded the gods of his fathers. The first step to godlessness is to turn away from the God of your parents. This is what Antiochus Epiphanes did. He was always brought up to believe in a god called Apollo. When he grew up he began to worship Jupiter the god of war, the god of fortresses described here. He certainly managed to attack and defeat many fortresses. There was another favourite god, this time worshipped by the women. Tenos or Adonis was the Greek name for this handsome young god, and you can read about this one and the women who worshipped him in Ezekiel 8:14. Antiochus would have nothing to do with that deity and he forbade the women of his kingdom to worship Adonis. Everybody had to worship his god – that was his first step. Then, gradually, he progressed from that to sharing the divine honours with Jupiter. Then, finally, Antiochus Epiphanes was saying, "I am Theos. I am god, and every coin in the realm must call me god, and every time people spend a coin at the shops they are spending a coin of god."

So in fact, vv. 36–39 do describe Antiochus Epiphanes. On the other hand, there are things in this verse that seem to go beyond anything he did, to some terrible blasphemy – to the point where he would acknowledge no other gods, and this

Antiochus never did as far as we know from the historical record. But I tell you now that in the double fulfilment that there is going to arise in our world, a world dictator. He will not only destroy all religions, and he will not only encourage worship of the state as happens in totalitarian countries today, he will finally reach the point where he will say, "There is only one god and I am that god and you bow down and call me lord." That is going to happen. It happened in the days of the Roman Empire when the Caesars took the title of "lord", and simple Christian people were thrown to the lions rather than say, "Caesar is lord", because their creed was "Jesus is Lord". I remember reading of a young mother who had just given birth to a baby and they arrested her because she was a Christian, and they put her in one cell and there was a barred window connected to the next cell and they put her baby in that cell. The baby cried for the mother's milk and the mother's breasts were longing to give that milk, and they said, "You can have your baby and feed your baby the moment you say, 'Caesar is Lord'." The mother stood firm and the baby died crying for milk, but the mother refused to say "Caesar is lord." She said there is only one Lord and that is Jesus. I can imagine few worse tortures than that for a woman, yet she stood firm, and what we are saying now is that this kind of situation is going to arise again at the end of history amongst those who still want to call Jesus or Yahweh "Lord" when this man Antichrist arises.

God's people were not protected from this before. They had to stand firm and they will have to do so again. So vv. 36–39 look at Antiochus Epiphanes and see in him the shadow of a greater tyrant yet to come – a man who will claim to be a deity. So with v. 40 we have moved on to the actual end of history. We are now beyond things that have happened.

We are now discussing a Middle East situation, which

will be the last world war. I have no doubt where the last world war will be, nor from these verses have I doubts about which areas of the world will be drawn into it. There is to be at least one more world war. This is it. There may be others first, but this is the very last one. It has no fulfilment in the days of Antiochus whatever; nothing in history corresponds to vv. 40–45 so we are way ahead now. We may live to see it, and if we do we shall see every detail and understand. This is at the time of the end. Why have we jumped over two thousand years? Why has the Bible slid so smoothly from Antiochus to Antichrist, from 165 BC when Antiochus died, right through to whenever this paragraph will be fulfilled? The answer is very simple: that Daniel's prediction is about the Jews, not the Gentiles, and there is a gap in Jewish history. They turn down their Messiah, and as far as God was concerned, the Jewish clock stopped ticking. It is only at the end of history that they come back into God's purposes, and we Gentile believers and God's ancient people will be grafted together again into one plant for God's glory, and there shall be one flock, one fold, one Shepherd, and it will be the Messiah of Israel, our Lord Jesus Christ. So the gap is explicable, and while they have been wandering around the world these last two thousand years, Israel has been out of God's plan – it is the tragedy of their history – but not out of God's heart. Read Romans 9–11. What a picture that gives of the fact that when God calls people he never lets them go. His calling is without repentance. He doesn't go back on it.

Let us look at the fulfilment of this last world war. Again Syria and Egypt (north and south of Israel) are the main protagonists. They are no longer allies in this picture. Israel lives in the corridor between Europe, Africa, and Asia, in that narrow strip of land which is the way through for all invading forces. If you go to Lebanon today there is a little river by the coast, and on the face of the rock by the river every world conqueror that has passed through this corridor has carved his name. You can read world history off that rock. They have all scratched their names on it as they came and went – right through to Napoleon. Israel is caught in the corridor of power politics, so the final world war is going to be in the Middle East and it is going to arise because Syria and Egypt will fall out with each other. It is going to arise because Syria will be much more powerful than she is today, probably helped by forces from the north. That could be ominously significant, but here we have the rise of the final world ruler, and as far as I can understand my Bible it is a real possibility that the final tyrant will be an Arab.

I am not going to go into further details except to point out that the ruler in the north will attack Egypt, will bring Libya in and Ethiopia, the whole northeast corner of Africa will come under his dominion, and then we find the news from the north causes him concern. He has to come back over. News from the north I think could hardly mean any other than Russia, and the book of Revelation tells us that the news from the east is that an army of two hundred million men is coming across the river Euphrates.

Where could such an army come from? There is only one country in the world that could mobilise that number and it is China. News from the north and the east, big powers coming into this conflict, will cause this tyrant to reverse from his African conquests and come back and pitch into the centre of world history between Jerusalem and the Mediterranean. It is so detailed. The Bible also predicts elsewhere that the final battle of the final world war will take place at a little hill guarding the western entrance to a triangular plane called the plane of Esdraelon. There the little hill of Megiddo (or Armageddon), with the ruins of Solomon's Stables on top of it, looks out over a plane which Winston Churchill called "the cockpit of the Middle East".

In fact, during the Second World War Churchill sent out a special group of British officers to survey that valley so that they could plan the final battle, because he thought the British Army was going to be trapped there between the Germans coming down through Greece and the Italians coming along from North Africa. He was wrong in his timing but he did know his Bible. So we can see the whole picture building up, but the last verse in the chapter tells you that this tyrant's days are numbered. When God has decided what is going to happen there is nothing a man can do to stop it, and when God has decided a man will die and be defeated and destroyed, then nothing whatever can stop that.

You can read a fuller account of this in Revelation chapter 19, where that final battle is described. It is therefore understandable that (in Daniel 12, and Daniel didn't bother with chapter numbers—somebody has put those in a thousand years later) the next verse goes straight on to say there will be trouble for Israel such as Israel has never seen.

One of the most intriguing little details given at this point is that the lands of Moab, Ammon and Edom will escape this holocaust. Of course, the Bible gives the names of those areas in Bible times so that they understood. What is the name of those three areas today? The name is very simple: Jordan. Everything east of the Jordan river – these are the areas of Moab, Edom, and Ammon, which indicates fairly clearly that what happened before will happen again, that the kingdom of Jordan will escape this and not be involved; that when Syria and Egypt are fighting one another, then Jordan stands by. It is remarkable how relevant this is, and how believable it is to us now.

In that very crisis we have the deliverance of the prince of the angels who watches over Israel: Michael. Have you been to Coventry Cathedral? Have you seen that magnificent statue by Epstein outside the main door, of Michael the angel towering above Satan, the defeated prince of this world? I hope the people who walk by and see that statue understand the message. I hope they know Daniel 12:1, because that is what it is all about.

We believe in angels, we believe that there is a guardian angel of nations, and there most certainly is a guardian angel of Israel. The very forces of heaven will come into that dreadful holocaust of the third world war. Yes, there will be suffering for Israel – big trouble. The time of "Jacob's trouble" it is called by another prophet, and one trembles for poor little Israel. They have had so much and they have not had the worst yet, but at the very lowest ebb of their fortunes, when the nation seems to be trodden underfoot by men, and it seems as if all is lost, and their nation is about to be obliterated and sink into the sands of time, Michael arrives, and he is more than a match for any human general.

That is what is to happen, and so they are to be redeemed. Many of them will have been killed, but we are told here that God has written many of their names in his book and that they will survive and be saved and redeemed. You know, the most important thing is that you should be sure that your name is written in God's book. When the roll is called, rejoice that your name is written in the Lamb's book of life. There are Jewish names in that book and they will survive the holocaust and they are going to be redeemed.

How? We know from a later prophet, Zechariah, that their very Messiah with his pierced hands will come to them at the crisis and they will look on him whom they pierced, and they will know *he* is their Saviour, not the Antichrist. Their Christ is the one to whom they must look. It only takes one thing to turn a Jew into a Christian and that is an encounter with the living Jesus. They have got the rest, and as I have seen Jewish people come to the Lord it has struck me again and again that as soon as they meet the risen Jesus they know more than I do. It is marvellous to see it.

I remember a Jewish girl coming to me after a service at which I had preached. She said, "Do you really mean that Jesus is our Messiah?"

"Yes," I replied, and spoke to her about this. She accepted him as the Messiah in the little vestry of that chapel. You know, immediately I felt she was way ahead of me in understanding. Saul of Tarsus had got it all, but he had never before met the risen Jesus and didn't believe he was alive – but when he met him on the Damascus road he saw it all. His theology, in a sense, was formed in that moment. He saw the church as the body of Christ in that moment. Why persecute me? But I didn't persecute you? Yes you did. This is my body. It all came to him in a flash. He could see it all. So when the Jews see Jesus, those who are still alive after this holocaust will be redeemed and accept him and become our brothers and sisters in Christ. What a moment!

What is the next thing that is going to happen? It is resurrection, for when Jesus comes back, the dead in Christ will rise – not just dead Christians but those who have believed before Christ, those who believed in God's words, that is when they will rise too. So Daniel, being spoken to about the Jews, is not told all believers will arise. He is told that many will arise, referring to the Jews. Many of the Jews who are dead and buried will arise that day. Not all of them, because not all of them have been believers, but many of them have been. You can read about some of the outstanding heroes of faith in Hebrews 11 – and many of them who are dead at that point and buried, will arise. We shall be there. What a meeting! Jews and Christians – believers united at last before the Messiah. I believe that this is what the Bible calls the "first resurrection" of dead Christians and dead believing Jews together.

There is a translation that we need to get rather carefully

here. The English usually says, "Many will arise, some to this and some to that," but in fact the Hebrew is, "Many will arise these to this" – not "some", *these*; the rest does not say they will arise at that time but it says what they will arise *to*. There is a resurrection for good and bad. Don't think death is the end for anyone. Whether you are a believer or an unbeliever – you will rise from the dead. But if you are a believer you share in that first resurrection and rise to everlasting life. If you are not, you will rise to everlasting shame and in contempt and you will have to live with yourself forever. That is sheer hell. The shame of it – that you had an opportunity to respond to God and you shut yourself off from the light and lived in darkness because your works were evil. The Bible is so clear: it always puts the word "everlasting" against both heaven and hell. In the parable of the sheep and goats (Matthew 25), Jesus talks about eternal punishment and eternal blessedness. Here Daniel makes the same point. Let us never dare to question the Word of God here: everlasting life; everlasting shame. You can't get around such language, horrible though it may be to our thinking – it is there as clear as it could be.

So resurrection, and then, following resurrection: reward. You know, whenever we want to make somebody look glorious we cover them with jewels. Go and see the crown jewels in the Tower of London. We put jewels on our royalty to make them glorious. In ordinary clothes they look ordinary people, but I tell you this: in the heaven of heavens when the people rise, some will shine without jewels. They will just shine gloriously. Who will shine? We talk about stars – film stars, pop stars – but I would rather glitter there than glitter here, wouldn't you? In fact, who will glitter? Those who have turned many to righteousness. Not just those who have lived right themselves, but those who have led others to do so also. The ones who will shine are not just those who manage to live a good Christian life themselves but those who have shared that life with others, and we shall get some surprises in that day. Some who may not be noticed in their church and have just quietly gone about turning others to righteousness, will shine on that day like the stars of heaven, so there will be reward.

We have got to the end of the vision and the prophecy. There are now some very practical things. There are some questions being dealt with. "Daniel ... the words are closed up and sealed until the time of the end." It is not to be published yet. This is the amazing thing: that many parts of the Bible as we have it were not written primarily for the day in which the writers lived. They were written down then so that we, two thousand and more years later, could read them and draw strength from them. You will find that there are parts of the Bible that come into their own in other circumstances. Could we be the generation for whom this book was written? It is an exciting thought, isn't it? Daniel was told the words are closed up and sealed, but sealing only closes for a time. That seal was broken in the time of the Maccabees, incidentally. Judas Maccabees read this vision and it spurred him on to fight against Antiochus Epiphanes and free Israel from that tyrant's power.

What Judas did then, Michael the archangel will do later. But let us ask about the other meaning of the word "seal": it is that this document is complete and must not be tampered with. It must not be altered; it must not be added to in any way. The devil is so rampant that Bibles have been printed in English which have tampered with the book of Daniel and have added chapters to it. Did you know that? Without realising this, you may have bought one of those Bibles, but I tell you the prophecy of Daniel is sealed. Look and see if there is a Daniel chapter 13. If there is, you have bought the wrong Bible. The Jerusalem Bible has it, the New English

Bible has added apocryphal books in one of its editions, and the Common Bible of the Revised Standard Version has done the same. If you read the unedifying rubbish of Daniel 13 of some Bibles, you will realise why the angel Gabriel said to seal the prophecy. Don't buy a Bible with apocryphal books. If you are interested in them, buy them in a separate book. They should neither be bought nor sold as part of the Bible; they are not the Word of God.

Until I gave the teaching on Daniel on which this commentary is based I had never before taken a congregation through the book of Daniel. At that time I had been twenty-five years a minister. I had preached on texts from it and little bits of it, and something had held me back. Then, eighteen months before the time came to teach it, God said to me, "Now give this book." I just had to get on with it, and I had no idea then that when I was teaching on it we would be living in the midst of a Middle East crisis. But that was what happened and it shed light on that.

So Daniel closed the book, and then the angels are puzzled too. There were three of them, remember, in chapter ten. Here they are again: the middle one is standing above the river, there is one on either bank, and they are puzzled and they are asking questions.

In 1 Peter 1:21 it says, "Even the angels long to look into these prophecies and decide what they are all meaning." So the angels are studying the prophecy as well as people like us. One angel says, "How long is this going to be? How long will Daniel's people suffer? How long will they go through this?" The angel Gabriel, with hands uplifted before God, swears on an oath, "It will be a time, times, and half a time." We know from other passages of the Bible what that means: a year, two years, and half a year. Do you know that six times in the Holy Bible God tells us in different ways that the time of this trouble will be three and a half years, forty-two months, one thousand two hundred and sixty days. He couldn't have made it more clear. Jesus himself said that God has shortened that time or nobody would survive.

So God has limited it to just three and a half years. At this point, Daniel has a question. He wants to know more. He doesn't understand this three and a half years. What will the issue be? What will happen after that? What will it all lead to? The angel's reply means, "Daniel you've got enough. That's all you need to know." The angel gives two little hints: 1,290 days after that trouble begins; and 1,335. In other words, after the three and a half years there is going to be something that will take one more month: something, another month and a half. What? I haven't a clue. I am just looking forward to the first month after Jesus gets back. Then I will look forward to the next six weeks and then I am just going to shout Hallelujah! Blessed are those who survive to the one thousand three hundred and thirty-fifth day. As much as to say: when Jesus comes back it will take him a little time to get his government established and get it all sorted out. So maybe another month, then a month and a half, then blessed. It is just a matter of months then, and God's kingdom is set up.

Oh what a time that will be! I have heard saints say, "I'm looking forward to the first five minutes after death." Well, we all are, but I am looking forward to the first month after the Second Coming to see Christ take the situation in hand and set it up. Antichrist will end at the end of three and a half years; another month and Jesus will have set his kingdom up and his government; another six weeks it will all be running smoothly, and we shall be praising the Lord and shouting hallelujah – that is my interpretation of it.

Daniel won't miss it. Isn't that a lovely touch at the end? "You will rest, and then at the end of the days you will rise to receive your allotted inheritance."

So the day I see Jesus, I will see Daniel – do you realise that? When Christ sets up his kingdom, I have no question as to one of the cabinet ministers who will be sharing in the administration, the man who through ninety years lived a faithful, godly life, the man who was prime minister of Babylon, the man who went on from one empire to another and was lifted to high office and who was a faithful civil servant here. I have no doubt that Jesus has a job for Daniel in his government when the government is on the shoulder of our Lord and Saviour.

I have missed out a verse, haven't I? I have not said a thing about v. 10. It tells me that the prophecies of Daniel will split people right down the middle into two groups, and two only: the wise and the wicked. The wicked will not understand and they will carry on in their behaviour exactly as they carried on before they heard the prophecy. The wise are those who understand and who change their way of living to prepare for what is to come, and who seek to lead others in the paths of righteousness.

We have been through the prophecy of Daniel now, into every verse, and have looked at the overall picture. I do not claim to have given you an infallible interpretation of every verse, and on some controversial matters there is room for honest differences of conviction and opinion, and we must mutually respect each other within the fellowship of Christ. But I believe that the broad picture I have given you is the picture that God wants us to have, and that this is going to divide congregations right down the middle. There are those who are in God's eyes wicked because they listen to it and their life afterwards is no different to the life they lived before and they see it as only an interesting intellectual exercise; and there are the wise who change and who lead many to righteousness. That is the qualification for understanding this book. Understanding God's Word is not a matter of your

IQ, not a matter of your intellect, it is a matter of your will. Those who are willing to be obedient shall know the doctrine and are the wise. Wise and wicked – two groups – and God has been dividing us through his Word.

For more of David Pawson's teaching,
including DVDs and CDs, go to
www.davidpawson.com

FOR FREE DOWNLOADS
www.davidpawson.org

Printed in the USA
CPSIA information can be obtained
at www.ICGtesting.com
LVHW012108270524
781518LV00031B/615

9 781911 173069